Rules for Roommates

Rules for Roommates

The Ultimate Guide to Reclaiming Your Space and Your Sanity

Mary Lou Podlasiak

Writers Club Press
New York Lincoln Shanghai

Rules for Roommates
The Ultimate Guide to Reclaiming Your Space and Your Sanity

Writers Club Press
an imprint of iUniverse, Inc.

For information address:
iUniverse, Inc.
2021 Pine Lake Road, Suite 100
Lincoln, NE 68512
www.iuniverse.com

ISBN: 0-595-12983-8

Printed in the United States of America

A special thanks to my husband,
even though he keeps dragging home stray cats,
and continues to throw my silk blouses
in the washer with his sweaty T-shirts.

Without his encouragement,
this project would still be a stockpile of paper scraps
jamming my desk drawers shut.

"To err is human; to blame it on the other guy is even more human."

—Bob Goddard

CONTENTS

FOREWORD

One wrong that can never be made right is the permanence of a personal attack on another human being in the literary world. I want to make my stance on that point perfectly clear before you howl in protest thinking one of my contributors is feeling giddy in having named you outright as the source of his or her distress. The motivation behind this project was simply to help roommates nurture and improve their relationships by examining typical grievances. All of the names have been changed to avoid embarrassment or regret on anyone's part.

Most reneged on pointing a finger before the final editing process anyway, admitting that there are always two sides to every story. And, as an afterthought, many participants chose to add more rules to the collection by repenting their own indiscretions, fearing rebuttals. Their admissions are a subtle reminder that no one is perfect, so when fed up with a cohabitant, we'll be careful to censor our own behavior as well.

PREFACE

The birth of this project occurred just as I was about to throw in the towel on a graduate studies assignment in counseling. The task was to examine potential conflicts in a platonic relationship of our choosing. Of course my classmates and I stampeded to the nearest bookstore in search of a topic that had already been thoroughly covered. The more exhausted the subject, the easier it would be to provide the groundwork for further research.

Finding what little had been written about this topic, I refused to be defeated. It seemed that everyone I came in contact with, from that point on, had something significant to say about this subject.

Social scientists can certainly put us on the right track when attempting to iron out relationship problems, but better yet, we can learn far more from people who have actually walked the walk, and talked the talk. The following opinions and accounts of those with first-hand knowledge about roommate relationships should help you self-diagnose, or better yet, prevent your own headaches.

INTRODUCTION

THE ONE THING WE ALL WANT

No matter what your circumstances may be, you probably have the same goal in mind as most people who share living quarters: You want your home to be a sanctuary where you can escape the pressures of the outside world. If you're typical, venturing out of your nest and into the public eye means succumbing to conformity. You behave quite well in order to keep from getting thrown out of restaurants, ostracized from social circles, or canned from your job. In fact, you'll put up with most any hassle if the alternative means you're apt to drive your career or reputation into a ditch. But returning home at the end of the day should mean more that just jumping off the hamster wheel — it should be something you look forward to.

Wouldn't it be marvelous to be able to shut out the rest of the world as you slam the door behind you, and then do exactly what you want to, without interference from others? You certainly have every right to a little peace, but the harsh reality is: *so does everyone else!* This is precisely why you'll never come close to creating a comfortable living environment that works for everyone, without establishing some rules and learning the art of compromise.

You can roommate-hop your entire life, in search of a trouble-free environment, or you can work at making a few adjustments and save yourself the inconvenience of all that packing. You're not the first person to have ever complained about wallowing around in the swill created by an undomesticated pig. Nor are you the first to have been bilked by a tightwad, robbed of sleep by a night owl, or agitated by a mental terrorist who can't seem to vent life's frustrations in the right direction: *Away from you.*

Whatever the alleged violation, when you feel you are being impositioned or mistreated, you probably have a valid complaint. The bigger the issue, the more confident we are that we have been wronged. But maintaining our sanity when minor infractions repeatedly occur can be tricky. It can get pretty tiresome having to ask yourself over and over again, *Is this something I should have the right to squawk about, or is it just me?*

How on earth did we become so nice that we have sacrificed our own well being by laying down and becoming nothing more than a doormat? For most of us, this conditioning to let the minor slights go, to steel ourselves against these day-to-day annoyances, started in a sandbox. As you were about to clobber the scoundrel swiping your shovel, adult intervention forced you to abort your mission and admit that you were somehow the twisted party. Then, compounding our parent's worries that we would become dysfunctionally self-absorbed, we became teenagers obsessed with peer acceptance. And as we grew into adults, we simply shut down to avoid complicating our already frenetic lives. If we didn't side-step every potential conflict, our lives would become nothing more than one continuous argument.

For those who have stumbled into the worst scenario, you are no doubt mentally banking each and every little incident, waiting in rabid anticipation of the next selfish act sure to come. Your level of distress has reached epic proportions, compounded by the guilt of having let yourself feel so out of control. Near the breaking point, you know if you explode into a tirade, you'll only shift the black hat to your head, causing the relationship to deteriorate even further.

We are much less likely to worry about hampering our self-image with family members or romantic partners. We can usually bank on unconditional love to smooth any ruffled feathers following a disagreement, making it easier to fight for what you want. This is the element that we have to learn to do without in platonic relationships. Still, in spite of such a gamble, you should never shortchange yourself by tolerating someone who is never able to accommodate or respect your wishes, family or not.

So why bother? Why not just live alone?

Some of us choose this lifestyle mainly out of economic necessity and look forward to the day when we can afford our own place. Others do it for emotional security. A roommate can enrich our social lives, offer support through turbulent times, and guard the fort while we're away. In some instances, it may even prevent someone from entering a marriage out of sheer loneliness, a lease that is not as easily broken. These are some of the simple reasons why we are willing to risk being taken advantage of.

THE TWO MOST IMPORTANT RULES

Most of the complaints throughout this book are about people who lack simple regard, those who always seem to put themselves first, oblivious to the burdens they place upon others. But, you may erroneously believe you are being trampled by such a narcissist if you continuously expect your roommate to read your mind. Not everyone is so egocentrically intense that they aren't willing to make a few adjustments to make others happy. The key is making your wishes known.

Only those who have a hankering for self-sabotage will ignore your requests. This doesn't mean that you should expect mandatory compliance the nanosecond you feel the whim to have things your way. If you lack the sensitivity necessary to accept the differences that set people apart, then you're the one who should be reprogramming your thinking.

With these thoughts in mind, you can choose between living a disgruntled existence or maintaining harmony by observing the two most important rules:

Don't expect your roommate to guess what you want,

and

Don't maintain that *your* way is the *only* way.

There is much to be learned from other people's conflicts and the action, or lack of, taken in each instance. Even if your problems prove to be unique, hopefully you will be able to carry away new insight to enable you to develop your own strategies for getting along. If nothing else, this

1

collection is bound to reiterate many of the same rules your parents demanded you follow while growing up, thus giving you the direction you may need while flailing around in an adult world without them.

JUST FOR DORMMATES

(BOOT CAMP FOR THE INEXPERIENCED)

This may be your first real encounter with cohabitation. Even if you drag a friend along to college, you'll soon learn that the challenge of living together has the potential to strengthen or break the bonds between you. You cannot count siblings in your repertoire of experience either. Why not? Because as kids, we co-existed with an entirely different set of rules. Drawing an imaginary line around the stuff you considered off-limits, and then threatening to beat the crap out of anyone crossing that border (except your mom), was totally acceptable. And for those of you who took a more civil approach when the fur began to fly, you probably ran screaming to the adult in charge to settle your disputes. You won't behave this way with your college roommate, *if you're smart*.

Yes, you'll definitely want this stranger to like you, and vice versa. Some college roommates remain friends for life, and you'll certainly want to keep that in mind in the event you are paired up with someone from Hawaii. (You'll want to start working right away on an invitation home for spring break.) Hopefully you didn't take any wrong turns when filling out your housing survey, but even if you didn't, don't be alarmed if you're not perfectly matched. Although most forms cover the basic issues, i.e., smoker vs. nonsmoker, there's nothing to cover personality conflicts. You might find yourself stuck with a social outcast who thinks you're the cat's pajamas and wants to become palsy-walsy. Or uglier yet, *you* may be the one who is shunned.

Hopefully you'll luck out, happily embarking on the whole college life experience side-by-side, accumulating memories of a lifetime. At some point; however, it is inevitable that you will mentally begin to accumulate a list of demands that you will carry into your adult life. You will learn what you can and cannot tolerate in another person. Your first roommate will probably get away with the most, especially now that your parents are no longer around to referee your squabbles, and you're not sure what is fair and what isn't.

Don't room with your best friend.

Why chance ruining a great friendship? Instead, request rooms on the same floor so you'll both meet new people and widen your circle of friends. You'll also have a place to run to when you need to get out of your room.

If you "click" with someone during college orientation, don't hesitate to ask that you be assigned to the same room.

This is a much better idea than risking being thrown in with the wolves. And most colleges will oblige you, considering the number of requests for room changes that will have to be dealt with when classes begin. After all, pairing up freshmen, after meeting special requests, becomes merely a lottery at some point for housing officials.

You should also consider the sizeable number of students who will withdraw at the last minute. Check out the people in rooms that have open beds.

"I nearly died when I walked into my room for the first time. There she was — a total burnout — a real hood from inner city. What she was doing at a religion-based school was beyond me. I lucked out when she lit up a cigarette in the hallway while we were moving in. Our resident assistant came shrieking down the corridor because there is absolutely no smoking allowed anywhere on campus. She packed up her car and went home the same day."

Rita

"My first experience was with a druggie whose parents sent her to a strict college to try to straighten her out. What she needed was rehab. Saying she was resistant to the rules would be putting it mildly. There were several other girls just like her, so it was easy to talk her into swapping so I could be paired up with someone more disciplined, like myself. Once I was honest about admitting I really didn't want to live with her, we became friends in a weird sort of way, and she still to this day affectionately calls me "The Church Lady."

Patricia Ann

Don't be an idiot and take up more than your share of available space.

If you lugged so much stuff with you that you can't confine it to your side of the room, then take it back home.

If something bugs you, say so from the beginning.

"I've always allowed myself to be trampled by other people, but I'm fussy when it comes to getting sleep. I started the conversation by asking if *I* had been doing anything that annoyed *her.* That paved the way for me to tell her nicely that she needed to stop running in and out of the room when I was trying to sleep."

Terri

Above all else, respect your roommate's desire to study.

After all, the reason most people shell out ten to twenty grand a year to attend college is to learn something. If you are there for some other reason, such as finding yourself, finding a soul mate, or partying on your parents' bankroll until you flunk out and have to get a job, then don't infringe on anyone's right to study while you are doing whatever.

"I'm in pre-med at a large university where it is dangerous to walk back and forth from the library at night. I can't afford to waste time waiting for someone from the campus escort service to show up, nor do I want to. So, I try to study as much as possible in my room, but the mouth breather I share a room with makes it nearly impossible. She mindlessly chatters about everything from her clumpy mascara to all the partying she'll be doing the next weekend. How do you politely tell someone to *just shut up?*"

Liz

"The guy I lived with went berserk when he found out I couldn't study or sleep without the stereo on. It wasn't that big a deal. I simply rearranged the room so my headphones would reach my bed and desk. All you have to do is compromise a little."

Paul

Lock the door, even when you step out for only a minute or two.

"Wear your key on a chain inside your clothing, long enough that you can bend over and unlock your door without removing it."

Mariam Crandall
Retired Dorm Mother

You should hold yourself financially responsible for whatever is ripped off because *you* left the door unlocked. Unattended, unlocked dorm rooms are an open invitation for thieves. If caught in action, these perpetrators usually claim to be *looking for someone* or declare to have been asked to *pick up something* and gee, *must have gotten the room number right, but the buildings confused.*

"I envied my roommate's small-town, naivete except that I couldn't get her to keep our door locked. Then it happened. Someone stole all my textbooks and returned them to the bookstore for the cash. I felt bad about doing so, but I *had* to ask her for the restitution money. It was clearly her fault."

Anita

Keeping your door locked may prevent more than theft.

"I got along fine my freshman year, with Beth, until tragedy hit our dorm. We attended a large university right smack in the middle of a city, and two fourteen-year-old thugs hid in the shower and raped a girl who lived right down the hall from us. Up until then, it had never bothered me that our door was usually left unlocked.

After that happened, we were both scared to death and began locking up all the time. But, Beth can be irresponsible, so I found myself jumping up the minute she left the room to see if she had locked the door. Every once in a while she *did* forget and then we would fight about it. I felt she had little regard for my safety, and she said I was unreasonably paranoid. I networked until I found a scaredy cat like myself, and then moved in with her."

Mary Anne

Never purposely lock your roommate out.

"Ben and I had gotten along for a year and a half, mainly because nothing ever seemed to bother him. I guess he was tired of me waking him up because I had the bad habit of slamming the door and didn't realize it. But instead of telling me, he got really mad and locked me out of our room in the middle of the night when I'd gone down the hall to the bathroom. I spent the rest of the night in the lobby.

The next day I went straight to the university housing office and he was placed on disciplinary probation. He was so mad, he moved out and commuted an hour one-way for the rest of the quarter. I didn't care. I was paying for that room too."

Alan

"I took a big chance when I allowed the college to randomly choose a roommate for me. I could have roomed with someone from my hometown, but I wanted to make new friends. As luck would have it, I got a real winner. I would come back from class and find the deadbolt locked so I couldn't get in, even with my own key. She would yell for me to come back in about an hour because her boyfriend was there. Where was I supposed to go? I was paying for half that room. It just wasn't fair. And, even after she would finally let me in, the room smelled like sex. It was totally gross!"

Jan

If it's not yours, don't touch it.

"Gary's parents paid for his education. I struggled through with loans, grants, and campus work study, plus I worked my can off in a hot plastics plant during the summer. He would help himself to a change jar I hid in my desk, just to get a lousy can of pop. Most of the time that was the *only* money I had."

Dan

"One day I was sitting in class thinking the guy next to me had major B.O., and then I realized it was my shirt that smelled. Another guy in our quad ratted that Ralph was wearing my clothes on weekends when I went home, and hanging them back in my closet. Everyone hated him. He would disappear whenever we ordered pizza and then show up after we'd paid for it and help himself. The whole floor threw a party when he flunked out and didn't come back."

Ed

"It seemed that I was going through shampoo awfully fast. Then one day I noticed my shampoo bottle felt damp, and I hadn't showered all day. That's when I realized Toni was helping herself to my things without asking. I'm not good at confrontation, so I took the dirty route. I added a little color enhancer to the bottle. I'm a flaming red head and she's a blonde. I found a note soon after that said she had gone home for a couple of days because she was sick. When she came back, her hair had obviously been re-dyed."

Nance

"It's amazing how one little thing can destroy your friendship. Cathy had lived with me all through college, and during the spring semester of our senior year, I had an extremely hot date with the quarterback on the football team, but she ruined it for me!

This was back in the 60's when you teased your hair into a helmet. When I went to spray my hair, she had used the last of my hair spray. I still haven't forgiven her for ruining my date."

Barbie

"The first couple of times my mom sent me chocolate chip cookies, I offered to share them with the girls in my suite. For some reason, they believed my generosity gave them a license to help themselves anytime. I'm gutless, so I invested in a locked box rather than confront them."

Carol

Even if borrowing seems OK, use your head about it.

One advantage of dorm life over apartment life is that you don't have to dicker over who owes what on monthly bills. And better yet, you don't have to wait for someone to cough up his or her share of the money. On the other hand, you'll have your first experience with financial hassles if your roommate breaks you up by making a habit of borrowing things.

"I knew Ned was on a tight budget, but that wasn't my burden to carry. He and I were both electrical engineering majors, so he would make sure our schedules were identical every quarter so that he could use my books!

It drove me crazy because he would want to know what course I was planning on studying each evening, so he could use the books I wouldn't need. I never knew what I would want to study for sure; it would depend on the mood I was in or how fast I would be able to cover the material. I started taking all my books to the library or home for the weekend so he'd get the message.

He finally found a fool in the work-study program to photocopy every single page of my books. That's not what I wanted either, but at least he stopped pestering me."

Dan

"It suddenly occurred to me that I was running out of toiletries more frequently than usual. Then I noticed that Susie was using the same old bottles for what seemed like an eternity. I cured her by not replacing anything so I had to borrow her stuff for awhile."

Darlene

"I'm a great believer in saving the environment, but I had to switch to expensive aerosol deodorant because Peggy was constantly running out of her own and then using my roll-on. The thought of using it after she had run it all over her armpits gagged me."

Rosie

Clear any "pow-wows" to take place in your room in advance.

"I like to study on Friday nights so I can go to Saturday afternoon football games and then party the rest of the weekend. After a long day of classes, I'd really like to be able to study in our room rather than walk all the way across campus to the library. I've come back a couple of times and found a poker game going on in our room. I wish my suitemates would at least tell me ahead of time."

Ralph

"Sally *never* studies. She doesn't have to. She's majoring in recreation, and a monkey could get that degree. So most of her time is spent socializing. Maybe I'm just jealous, but people are constantly stopping by our room to see her. I hate it. I wish she would just take her friends down to the lounge so I could get some studying done in our room."

Katrina

Clear your plans for overnight guests. (And check dorm policies!)

A most considerate person would only invite an overnight guest for the rarest of occasions. Some campuses sponsor events such as "little siblings" weekend, where cramping what little space you have, for just one weekend, should be understandable.

If your roommate goes home every weekend, or sleeps elsewhere, then that's a different story. Just be sure to keep your "guest" out of your roommate's bed, unless you put your own sheets, etc., on it. Then put the bed back together, *exactly* the way it was.

"Brenda had a home-town friend that spent almost every weekend with us. Her parents were making her commute to save money, and she didn't want to miss any fun. At first, I was miffed because we were so crowded even without her. But, she made sure to make up for invading my territory. She brought me a huge bag of toiletries, snacks, and other really cool things from her father's drug store. That really saved me a lot of money, so I decided I could put up with just about anything."

Dee Dee

Never, under any circumstances, allow your lover to spend the night.

"Imagine my surprise when a girl down the hall, that I barely knew, flagged me down to tell me not to go into my own room! The shrew I roomed with had talked her into letting me stay in her room, without even asking me first. I waited until five o'clock the next morning and then I just about tore the door off of the hinges. She never pulled that again."

Lori

"I'm not exactly what you'd call assertive, but I found an easy way to solve the overnight boyfriend problem before it began. When Carla, who clearly lived life in a faster lane than me, asked, *You don't mind that Bud is coming for the weekend do you?* I just smiled and said, *This weekend would be fine because I'm going home.*"

Cindi

"I used to get nauseated listening to Bill and his girlfriend trying to have sex quietly in the dark while I was in the room. The next time you have sex, listen to yourself! There is *no way* you can be quiet while doing it."

Aaron

"Can anyone top the experience of having someone on the bottom bunk rocking the boat while you're trying to sleep? It's feels like you're riding one of those mechanical horses for little kids outside of a grocery store."

Roger

Don't be a tagalong.

Your roommate is not in charge of your social life. If you're starting out friendless, make sure you attend college orientation and attend campus mixers so you can meet people. These events are not always the nerd fests you envision.

"Charlie was one of those guys who just couldn't be helped, and I couldn't go anywhere without him tagging along. My friends thought he was nerdy, and the more he felt their rejection, the harder he tried to fit in. One night we were joking with a group of really hot girls on the street, and thinking he would impress them, he *whipped it out* and *swung it around*. One of them called the campus police on her cell phone, and we were all put on disciplinary probation.

A couple of times, I didn't even go back to the dorm after my Friday afternoon classes, just to avoid him. Then I started feeling bad because he knew I was ditching him. I forced myself to invite him now and then, but he eventually stopped accepting. To my relief, he requested a new room assignment at the end of the year."

Ric

Don't ask, "Where are you going?"

"I can't even run down the hall to the bathroom without being asked where I am headed. Jill is *so* afraid I am going to do something without her. The only club she has probably ever belonged to in her whole life is the 'No Cavity Club'. I like her, but I get sick of being around her all the time. Now I can see why couples need time apart, which has improved my relationship with my boyfriend."

Genny

Announce where you are going when you leave the room, even if it is a lie.

"It used to give me the willies when Sherri would put on her coat and take off somewhere. I didn't consider myself to be a nosey person, it's just that I felt weird that she would just get up and leave. She wouldn't say where she was going or how long she would be gone. If I knew she would be out for awhile, then I could plan on doing something that normally annoyed her, like playing country music or having my boyfriend over."

Joan

Don't slam the door.

Your mother knew what she was talking about. It is annoying when you're awake, and it is unforgivable when you're trying to sleep.

Wash your clothes.

Normal people wash their clothes after they've worn them once. If you work out or participate in sports, hang your sweaty clothes somewhere to dry before throwing them in with your other dirty clothes. Don't forget that you can throw most tennis shoes in the washing machine too.

"One night when I was visiting my sister on campus, we got a little tipsy. And then for fun, she started randomly pulling articles of clothing out of her roommate's closet to prove what a pig she was. She used a rating system on a scale of one to ten, to determine just how gross each piece was. Before long, we had a small crowd in the room, joining in the game, and laughing hysterically. I was scared to death she would walk in, but no one else cared. Can you imagine someone doing that to your clothes? I'd be mortified!"

Karen

Wash your sheets.

"I figured out that mine must be giving off an odor I couldn't smell when Jack offered to wash them for me. I had always heard that you can't smell your own body odor. Whoops."

Josh

"The dork I lived with my freshman year did not wash his sheets the entire first semester. When he left for Christmas break, I threw them in the dumpster and left a note on his mattress claiming to be a chick hot for his scent, who stole his sheets. That scum-bag believed that some bimbo really wanted those crusty rags."

Tom

Shower, wear deodorant, and brush your teeth daily.

"I could tell when Alice cut classes all day because she'd also skip her shower. Did she think I really didn't *mind* her stench?"

Reddy

"You will never know how relieved I was when my foreign roommate asked me to *Americanize* him. I immediately introduced him to good hygiene. In his country, pungent body odor is considered to be quite amorous."

Ned

If you have a stereo or boom box, buy and use a set of headphones.

When it comes to listening to music, few people are ever in sync. Even if you like the same type of music, there will be times when one of you will prefer not to listen to it. Some people like to sleep all night with music playing, some have the unbelievable knack of studying with background music on, and there are some people who are not happy unless they are blasting away all day long. If you own a headset, there shouldn't be any problem. You can buy cords that stretch all over the place. And, if someone wants to listen too, all you have to do is unplug your headset.

If you are a slob, practice giving a little order to your private space.

Why is it that Type A people always get stuck with Type B people messing up their lives? If you're Type A, then maybe it's time you draw that imaginary line down the middle of your room before things start spilling over into your territory. If you're Type B, you need to forget all those lame excuses you used at home for not cleaning up your rat's nest of a room. Let's face it, how hard can it be to keep a bed, desk, closet, and little floor space cleaned up?

The process is simple:

(1) Use bookends and a few containers to keep all of your study paraphernalia orderly.
(2) Buy a comforter for your bed. All you have to do is basically throw it on top of your crumpled sheets to look decent.
(3) Keep a box or laundry basket in the bottom of your closet and throw dirty clothes in it.
(4) Keep a box under your bed or in the closet to hold things you don't know what to do with.

"Our beds were low to the floor, but up high enough we could keep all of our shoes and other stuff under there."

Camellia

"We bought an extra trash can. That really helped curtail the mountain of pizza boxes we accumulated."

Max

"To get my roomie to clean up his side every once in a while, I'd tell him my mother, professor, or someone else of importance would be stopping by while he was in class."

Robert

"I used to think air fresheners were dumb because my grandmother had them stuck all over the house and it always smelled like a funeral parlor. Since we both played college basketball, that was the only way to fight the smell. We even stuck them in our shoes so when girls came over, they wouldn't gag."

Travis

If you choose to join a sorority or fraternity, conduct your *Greek* activities elsewhere.

There is tremendous potential for conflict in this area. The "rush" activities during which new members are lured into joining, can be slightly annoying to people who have absolutely no interest in Greek life. If you are the *joiner* in your room, don't subject others to the frequent visits and pranks that can come with pledging. Tell the organization your room is off limits.

Keep in mind that there may be more to this than your roommate's alleged indifference. He or she may not be able to bear the expense or time involved in belonging to a sorority or fraternity. And, once you join, you'll soon be making plans to move, and you'll no longer have time to socialize with "outsiders", and whomever you live with will be well aware of this fact.

"Kelly said we would still be friends, but after she joined, I couldn't even stand to go to the cafeteria with her. It was all she talked about! She acted as if she hated to leave me when she moved into the sorority house, but by then, I couldn't wait to get rid of her."

Maddy

Don't treat dorm-life like one continuous pajama party.

Staying up all night to socialize and then sleeping all day and skipping classes is your vested right, until you start keeping everyone else awake.

"You would think that Shelly would know that when I got into bed, laid down, and pulled the covers up, that I was ready to go to sleep. Instead, she thought it was time to talk and giggle like junior high school girls. She was one of those people who have a fully charged battery pack running her mouth continuously. There was absolutely no way to shut her up. I waited patiently, and sure enough, she finally flunked out."

Clara

"I was beginning to wonder if anyone on my floor was actually seeking a college degree. Everybody stayed up half the night running up and down the hallway, eating, blasting their stereos, and scream-talking. I finally moved to an honors dorm, which I had avoided in the first place thinking everyone would be boring misfits. They really weren't at all. They were just more mature and knew how to balance studying and socializing. We just horsed-around on weekends, which was more my speed."

Mary Jo

Do your own course work.

"At first, I was happy that the university placed me with another computer science major. I thought we could put our heads together and accomplish twice as much. Instead, I got a bum steer. He waits until I'm done with assignments, and then asks to see my work. I don't think he's stupid, he's just lazy."

Bill

"Thank God I was smart enough to realize what a conniver Jill was. She thought she was copying my psychology term paper, from the previous semester, word for word. Instead of giving her the original, I gave her a copy of a juvenile paper I had written in high school that I had kept for the sources. I don't think she even bothered to read it before photocopying it and turning it in.

She was furious when she received an F, but didn't tell me. Another girl on our floor relayed this information to me. Apparently Jill thought it was a 'safe' thing to do, merely because we had different professors. Doesn't she know their offices are side by side and they share graduate assistants who grade freshman level papers?"

Stacy

"During my sophomore year in college, two guys who lived together on my floor were caught cheating in our accounting class. During the final exam, one of them claimed to have forgotten his calculator, and expected the other to bail him out by sharing his. The calculator passed between them only one time before the professor threw them out of the test. It was quite a fiasco. They were subsequently dismissed permanently from the university.

I'll never forget seeing that as long as I live. And, now that I'm a teacher, I never miss an opportunity to tell that story to my seniors in hopes they will never buckle under the pressure to help someone cheat."

Peter

Don't expect free typing service because you were too lazy to take the course in high school.

"For some reason, Jeremy thought I should cheerfully type his papers for him just because I knew how and he didn't. Typing is not like sitting in a hot tub or eating a pizza. It's work! I wouldn't have minded so much if he would have paid me. What made it even worse was that he would sit there writing while I waited for him to finish a page so I could type it. I can't believe any idiot would sit through four years of high school and not take a keyboarding class, especially when he knew he was college bound."

Dell

If your roommate doesn't smoke, then don't smoke in your room.

When you filled out the questionnaire provided by the college housing department (if you bothered), how did you answer the question about smoking? If you lied and said that you're a non-smoker, because you knew your mother would see the form, then you screwed up. This is the one request you can count on college officials to give top priority to. Non-smokers do not get placed with smokers.

What if you choose to start this nasty habit? Moving away from home places you in an extremely vulnerable position, one in which you may experiment with a lot of new things. If you fall prey to this addiction, curtail it to places other than your room.

"Carly started smoking and drinking coffee to help her pull all-nighters before exams. She would open a window thinking that the small amount of ventilation would work for our room. Everything smelled putrid, including the clothes in my closet. Our room was just too small for someone to smoke without offending me, and the draft from the window started making me sick too. I had to move in the middle of the semester."

Sis

Before you live together for even a day, outline what you believe will be your daily routine for one another.

"I was class valedictorian, so I had excellent study habits. I wasn't about to compromise my normal routine because it had worked really well for me in high school. Every night after dinner, I would study until ten o'clock with a ten minute break every hour. Then, I would get up and study for an hour before my first class. I'm glad I asserted myself, because right from the beginning, Michelle would chase her friends off to someone else's room when they stopped by to see her."

Linda

"I was placed with a vocal music major who sang in our room, rather than trudge clear across campus to use a practice booth. At first I thought, *you've got to be kidding,* but then she suggested something to me that improved my concentration tremendously. When she sang, I donned my headphones and listened to her CD's of forest sounds and studied the sciences required for freshman. Normally, I hated these classes, but that really put me in the mood. Then my sophomore year, I got rid of that little song bird."

Sami

If you need advice about dealing with a problem, talk to your resident advisor in confidence. Don't blab your problems up and down the hallway to anyone that will listen.

Most resident advisors are upperclassmen, hired to enforce rules and settle disputes. They are the next best thing to having your mother around to complain to, only better. They have been college freshmen too, and have an idea of what you are going through. They may have something negative to say if you're caught wheeling a keg into the dorm, but in general, their own experiences have provided them with a wealth of information that could help you.

"I'd like to see the housing form I filled out before I started college. I must have accidentally checked the box where it said, *Check here if you want to live on a floor with immature lunatics.* They remind me of when I was in the sixth grade and the mean, popular clique of girls would choose someone to pick on mercilessly. That's what these girls are doing to me because the emotional cripple I live with rounded them up with crazy stories about how badly I have treated her. Everyone on our floor, but me, knows what I have done to upset her. Get me out of here!"

Ally

"Whenever someone comes to me with a problem, I usually end up giving the same advice over and over. You have to talk to the source of your problems or nothing will ever be solved. No one ever wants to hear that, but you can't expect someone to change if he or she is unaware there is a problem. It's all about compromise."

Sara, Resident Advisor

You're in college now, so act like it!

"The most frustrating type of student I have to work with is immature freshmen girls. I don't know how some of them survived high school. One complaint that will always stick with me was from a girl who said, *You should see the way she looks at me.*

I suggested she try walking around campus, and when she found someone who *looked* at her in a suitable manner, she should ask that person to move in with her. Then maybe she would be happy."

Sophie, Dorm Counselor

Accept the inevitability that you will have conflicts, or at least some tension, now and then.

"Jessie and I lived together throughout college. We never had any kind of fight except for once during our junior year. I contracted a horrific stomach flu, and she acted like a brat about it. All I needed was to sleep it off and she wouldn't let me. Instead of watching her afternoon soaps in the lobby as usual, she stayed in our room and drove me nuts. Then *she* got sick and expected special treatment from me. She asked me to go buy her some medicine and I hit the ceiling.

We carried on for days and threatened each other with moving out. The girls in our hall began complaining about the noise and stopped speaking to us. That's when we banned together and realized we were being silly to throw our friendship out the window over one stupid fight. We're still close, even though we now live in different cities."

Marla

"Every month, for about a week, I become a complete hormonal mess. Pat used to take my rantings and rotten moods personally and believed that she had somehow caused them. The only way I could relieve her of this self-inflicted guilt was to hang up a calendar on which I have high-lighted the days I will probably have intensive mood swings. She now finds this amusing, so the problem has been solved."

Bebe

Don't stew about a problem, learn to compromise.

"Sandy likes to stay up until the wee hours of the morning studying, but I can't sleep with even her desk light on. I also hate sleeping on the top bunk, but we had flipped for the bottom, and I lost. We negotiated and agreed to switch beds so that I could drape a curtain from the top frame and then she can leave a light on all night if she wants to. It's working out beautifully."

Tonie

"I knew Karen didn't like me the entire year we lived together, but I couldn't figure out why. Right before I left on summer vacation, she screamed that she hated me because I kept her awake playing my stereo all night, all year long. She had made herself miserable for nothing. I would have gladly turned it off if only she'd told me it bothered her."

Stacie

Accept the fact that some battles can't be won — so change your attitude about the situation, or move out.

"*I* moved out. I went home every weekend to see my boyfriend, and one time when I returned, I could tell that someone had been sleeping in my bed. It was obvious that whoever it was had had sex, and had been in a smelly bar. Talk about gross. When I confronted Karen, she flippantly replied, *So what! You weren't here*! Then I stayed up half the night washing my bedclothes.

The next weekend, I came back to find that this time, they had done *it* on top of my satin comforter! I complained about that, and she said I was anal. And, the following weekend, I carefully laid out a sweater on a towel to dry to keep her off of my bed. Unbelievably, I returned to find my sweater thrown haphazardly over top my closet door.

That was it. The quarter was almost over and I was moving out. The very last weekend I was away, I stripped my bed completely before I left. When I returned, I could smell the same unmistakable odor on the mattress and my bare pillow. Now she was doing it to drive me crazy.

When I moved out, I freaked out and tore open my pillow and dumped the foam stuffing all over her side of the room. After all, it was such a small request to stay off of my bed, but it was the principle of the whole ordeal that set me reeling in the end."

Paula

If you don't like whom you've been paired up with, find someone else.

The marvelous thing about living in a dorm is that it is a fantastic place to practice getting along with someone, yet it can be as temporary as you want it to be.

You don't have to sign a lease that comes with apartment life, lasting a minimum of a year, sticking you with the same person. If you're desperately unhappy, simply go to the director of housing and ask for a new room assignment. It's that simple. However, you could be thrown in with another dysfunctional stranger, so it would be wise for you to try and find someone on campus in the same boat who is more suitable for you before asking to move. The bigger the campus, the better. Ask to be moved to another building if possible.

"Fred left our windows open night and day, and old dorms do not have screens. He left a jar of honey open on his desk and a swarm of bees filled our room while we were at class. After a brief stay at the hospital, I requested a new room assignment. I got one before the swelling went down!"

Norm

Take the grownup approach and be willing to discuss conflicts. If this courtesy is not returned, then refuse to allow yourself to feel guilty.

"Nancy would rather run down the hall telling anyone who will listen what I've done wrong, rather than tell me. To me, she is less of a person for doing that, than for not confronting me in the first place. I'm through with her pettiness. I'm moving out."

Anne

"Pete was an intolerable psycho. He wouldn't speak to me for days at a time when he was mad at me for some stupid reason, like waking him up when I came in late. It became impossible for me to study because the silence was deafening."

Ron

If it is clear that you are disliked and your efforts to become friends have become futile, then give it up and get on with your life.

Once again, we can blame the infamous questionnaire you mailed in before your arrival on campus. There really isn't a better way to try and match you up with someone you are likely to hit it off with. But sometimes this method is not much better than drawing names out of a hat. Humans are far too complex to second-guess compatibility by linking people according to interests alone.

"I know why Shelly and I ended up together. She check marked the box *I like sports* on her personal profile. I play college basketball and she likes to watch Nascar on television, which in my book doesn't even qualify as a sport. Anyway, she carries on about my smelly gym clothes. Well, excuse me, but how to you play basketball without sweating?"

Beth

When your roommate is consistently less than amicable, why bother kissing up when you could be out there making friends with people who are instantly receptive to you? *That* is how you find a good match.

Most people appreciate honesty, and will respect you for it. However, there is a fine line between being honest and being brutal. Know the difference.

"I changed rooms because the fat, lazy slug I was paired up with did nothing but eat and study. I couldn't stand the sight of him and I told him so. In retrospect, I regret being so nasty, and fate duly punished me for this error in judgement. The string of guys I went through after him drove me out of my gourd because I never got any peace. He wouldn't have been any trouble at all if I'd respected his laid-back lifestyle and wouldn't have been so concerned with having a wild social life."

Bennie

Collectively, guys seem better able to avoid putting up with much guff, but it is no wonder with the undaunted heroes our society promotes through the media. Mimicking those tough male images is not always necessary or appropriate, especially when your opponent is already on the mat.

"I was totally cruel for badgering Ed to tell me whether he was flunking out or not. I was concerned with myself, worrying about whether or not I would be getting a new bunkmate the next quarter. He ended up half dead in his parent's garage. They found a rag stuck in the tailpipe of his dad's car. I didn't realize the pressure his parents were putting on him and I was only making it worse."

Fred

Sometimes you need to just look out for number one. Don't be afraid to move out if it is in your best interests.

People who are self-assured and direct when confronted with trouble-some behavior are not to be envied, but to be copied. You have the right to look after yourself, and should do so.

"In my case, the need was extreme. I stayed long enough to learn that he had his own arsenal, including a homemade bomb. Who knows what he thought he was going to do with all that stuff. I told the housing director I hadn't intended to join the Army. I didn't just ask to change rooms, I asked to change dorms!"

Tom

"I regret taking the coward's way out instead of telling the simple truth. Like most women, I've been conditioned to do and say *the nice thing*, but I got caught in my lie. I created an elaborate story about how I would be transferring to another university, when I was really moving into a single room across campus. Her incessant chattering was cutting into my study time. Then I'd planned on telling her I'd changed my mind when I ran into her on campus.

The day after I moved, she showed up at my door with a dictionary I'd left. Apparently my mother had called earlier and blown my cover without me knowing it. I felt like such a fool for lying."

Katrina

Don't be offended when an old college roommate fails to keep in touch.

Having a great relationship doesn't necessarily mean you will remain friends for life. Some people see graduation as the "final chapter" in their college lives. They may see no point in maintaining a long-distance friendship, and if it makes you feel any better, the majority of college graduates also shun invitations to alumni events. So don't take it personally when you call, write, or visit and get the cold shoulder.

Some people simply like to get on with their lives and invest their energy and free time in whomever they are connected with at the moment. Others may reject your attempts to form a life-long alliance because they merely detest the work involved. Writing letters or returning phone calls are drudgery. Reciprocating your correspondence is just one more addition to a "should do" list that hangs over the head of any career-minded person.

If you didn't spar while you lived together, then you shouldn't assume that you are a painful memory. Unless you lived with a pro at masking discontent, your ex-roommate has cut the umbilical cord between you for the aforementioned reasons, or for the same reason people skip their high school class reunions: They have become fat, bald, or unsuccessful and you haven't.

FIGURING THE ODDS

(THINGS TO CONSIDER BEFORE YOU
STICK THAT KEY IN THE DOOR.)

Part of the fun of growing up is looking forward to those milestones like wearing your first bra and getting your driver's license. When you finally have the freedom to choose whom you'll live with, you will have truly crossed the threshold into adulthood. At this point, you're probably an upperclassman, or ready to enter the world of work, or you've gone berserk living with your parents and can finally afford to make the move.

But beware — the Pollyanna in you may be dictating your rational thinking. You're all grown up and about to live with another grownup, so you'll get along like big people should. Right? Well maybe, unless you harbor the false expectation that you'll be instantaneously compatible.

You may or may not already have a vague idea of what you want, or you may not know until you don't get it. Just remember that everyone is raised in a different environment. Even with similar backgrounds, such as socioeconomic levels and urban-versus-city upbringings, you'll each exhibit routines and habits that may seem foreign to one another. Hopefully, you'll keep an open mind and view any quirky behavior as entertainment rather than an infringement.

Check out the habitat before you move in.

"I really needed a place to live, but I wish I would have taken more time and been more selective. I agreed to move in with a girl at work before I saw her apartment. It was so dirty I had to wipe my feet on the doormat when I went back outside!"

Sabrina

"Right before we moved in together, I visited Terri's apartment. Junk was stacked everywhere, dirty clothes covered the floor, and dust was a half-inch thick on any surface that didn't have something piled on it. It was a relief when she claimed she had let the place go knowing she was moving soon.

After about a month together, she said she *just couldn't get to it.* Then she became engaged and said that when she got married, she *would have time to keep things nice.*

We're still friends now that she's married, but she is still an absolute pig, and at least *I* don't have to live with her anymore."

Teresa

"Jeff's apartment was spotless when I moved in, which thrilled me to the bone, but now I'm miserable. I feel like I'm living with my grandmother because he won't even let me put my feet up on the coffee table."

Noah

Don't think you'll get along because you are both slobs. Eventually, someone will have to clean up.

"I drove the first girl I lived with up the wall because she was such a raging cleaning fanatic, so for my second venture, I looked for just the opposite. Now I'm the one going crazy because neither one of us wants to clean up anything. There are never any clean dishes, the bathroom is covered with mold, the whole place stinks to high heaven, and I even have roaches crawling all over my bed."

Naomi

Be wary of living with a divorcee who has child visitation rights.

"I felt sorry for Jeremy because he took his divorce so hard. I truly had every intention of helping entertain his two kids when they came to visit every other weekend, but that got old real fast. They tore up the apartment while he was slouched in front of the TV, totally ignoring them. No wonder his wife wanted rid of him. Now, I do too."

Nathan

"Robert must have been trying to get the Father of the Year Award. Whenever his kids came to visit, I wasn't permitted to drink a beer, have my girlfriend over for the night, or watch anything on television except non-violent cartoons. I had to move out so I could be a grown-up again."

Tom

"I got tired of Jenny's little girl sneaking into my room and getting into my makeup and jewelry. After tangling up my gold chains and smearing half a tube of lipstick all over her face, she paraded into the living room and her mother just tee-heed about it. I put a lock on my bedroom door, which was a pretty obvious thing to do, so then it was *she* that broke our lease and moved out, costing me a bundle in the end."

Monica

Carefully consider a big age difference.

"Looking back, I should have been able to predict some of the problems we're having because of the vast difference in our ages. She's 25 and I'm 38.

For about the first 30 years of my life, I wanted to be popular and important like she does. But most people eventually reach the point at which I'm at now — they just want to be left alone to relax after work, not live in an environment where the phone and doorbell are constantly ringing."

Sally

"I was subjected to listening to an oldies station on the stereo, but worse than that, he thought he knew a hell of a lot more than I did about everything. I got sick of his unsolicited advice like how to keep track of the fuel efficiency on my car. I was still at that irresponsible stage when you're getting drunk and running your car into a ditch."

Adam

"I could have given birth to Annie, yet like an idiot, I still agreed to share an apartment after my divorce. What a mistake!

The first day, I got glass in my foot because she broke a bottle and half-ass cleaned it up. She stays out partying all night, wakes me up when she comes home, and then asks me to call her off work the next day. Now, she has foolishly become engaged and makes me a nervous wreck cheating on the poor guy.

I'm keeping my mouth shut so hopefully they'll get married and I can get rid of her."

Alexis

Don't move in with someone who is dating your boss.

"I might as well go to work and pull my pants down in front of my boss, because I know Angie tells him every intimate detail of my life. Maintaining a professional image at work is next to impossible knowing he is probably snickering behind my back about my plowing into the mailboxes with my car, or catching an oven mitt on fire. How do I have a chance for advancement with him knowing all my personal inadequacies?"

Bobbi

"Mindy dates a man who is in a higher position than me in our company. Unbeknownst to me, she was using me for information about other employees to help him. I thought she was just enjoying idle gossip with me. There were repercussions at work because of my stupidity, and it was obvious who squealed. I'm looking for another job and another apartment on the other side of the city, and I dread having to make a new circle of friends."

Sharon

"Try calling in sick when your boss comes out of your roommate's bedroom in the morning!"

Brianna

If you are widowed, divorced, or recovering from a failed relationship, don't jump into something else too fast!

"After Harry died, I thought I couldn't live alone for 5 minutes, so I allowed some old coot to move in. You know the type. I'm sure he scanned the obituaries looking for an old washerwoman, and now I'm it! Why didn't I just date around for awhile and find some nice gentleman who would drive me around and buy me nice things?"

Rosa

Steer away from choosing someone who is intellectually superior if you are insecure by nature.

"Sally is the manager of a salon, which I feel is a highly respectable profession, but she has an inferiority complex because I hold a master's degree in education. She recently accused me of trying to make her feel dumb in front of her boyfriend, who is an accountant, because we sometimes engage in conversations of which she knows little about. If she would just watch the news or read a newspaper once in a while, she would know what we're talking about and would be more interesting to him. It's obvious she can't converse on his level, but he's in love with her big boobs and gorgeous looks and doesn't care. Plus, he gets free haircuts.

I feel like I have to hide whenever he's around because he likes to talk to me and it makes her furious."

Carla

"One evening Roger suggested we play a trivia game with our friends, and it was embarrassingly obvious that he had been memorizing the cards on the sly. I hadn't realized how intellectually inferior I made him feel, and I believe it is simply because I graduated from college and he quit after his freshman year."

Scott

"Carrie has a Ph.D. in nursing, and I never attended a day of college in my life, but we get along famously. She might have a formal education, but I'm proud of the fact that I'm self-educated. I read voraciously and watch public television, so I actually feel as if I know more than she does."

Tommie

When your boss, a relative, or a friend asks you to take in someone as a personal favor, don't do it!

"Thanks to my big mouth, my boss found out I had a three bedroom apartment and lived alone. He asked if his daughter could move in with me. She was moving to town and didn't know anyone.

I foolishly believed she would make friends and soon want a place of her own, with her own things. Instead, she was perfectly content to use all my stuff, and didn't seem to notice or care about the extra wear and tear on my furniture.

I ended up in a bad marriage, and looking back, it was just to get out of this arrangement gracefully without losing my job."

Amber

Don't harbor the notion that just because you are moving in with someone, you will automatically become best friends.

"I found out the hard way that cohabitation doesn't insure trust. The first few days Pheobe and I were together, we stayed up late talking about ourselves, and I revealed way too much about my past. I was mortified to learn she had disclosed every detail to her boyfriend and family. At first I wanted to maim her physically for betraying my confidence, but then I realized it was my own fault. It was silly of me to believe I would be guaranteed confidentiality just because we lived together."

Toni

"A friend of mine called to confirm that she had made the hotel reservations at the beach for our annual vacation together. Sue went nuts because I hadn't included her."

Cindy

Be prepared to risk your friendship if you move in with a good friend.

You would think that living with a good friend would be an ideal situation. It certainly makes sense to move in with a constant companion, simplifying your social life. But once in while, as with all seemingly predictable life events, you might be fooled. People change, and so do circumstances.

"Hanging out together and living together are two entirely different things. After about a month, I decided Haley had been secretly raised by a pack of wolves. She had filthy living habits, and worse yet, she was instantly possessive of me. She couldn't stand for me to make plans with anyone else, knocking everyone I came in contact with."

Marie

"Ron and I roomed together all through college and were inseparable, except for dating now and then. After graduation, we landed jobs in the same city, so naturally it followed that we rented our first apartment together.

He fell hard and fast for a girl he met at work, and she still lived with her parents, so she was at our place every night and all weekend. I suppose he thought I didn't mind because she cooked a lot and cleaned for us, but I got sick of her anyway.

His parents called and said they were coming in on Saturday morning, and I purposely didn't tell him. The scenario was worse than I'd imagined. I let his parents in and you could hear his bed banging against the wall and his girlfriend squealing.

He said he'd give me 24 hours to move out or he'd throw my stuff in the street. In retrospect, I'd say that was generous."

Shawn

"We were in college and barely old enough to drink when Peggy, Sue, and I rented our first apartment together. To heck with dorms rules! We could have parties and friends over whenever we wanted!

At first, it was exactly that. Three friends living together had panned out to be everything we had imagined. At least until Peggy's mother was diagnosed with terminal cancer.

It wasn't the kind of cancer where you hope and pray for a miracle. It had taken over everything, including her daughter's sanity. Sue and I committed ourselves to be there for our friend whenever she needed us. And we were at first, but it was not enough for Peggy.

She began to misdirect her anger at me. Sue stayed busy and out of sight, but Peggy and I ran on parallel schedules because we were both in the same major. She began to pick at everything I said and did, and undermined me to our professors and friends at school. She betrayed confidences I had revealed long ago, embarrassing me to no end. It became a nightmare I couldn't wake up from.

A couple of months following her mother's death, the situation had clearly not improved, so I bailed out and transferred to another college. I broke the lease, also destroying my friendship with Sue because we lost our security deposit and she claimed she had no where to go. Now she and Peggy were a united front against me.

I told them to let me know what they thought would be a fair amount to settle the difference in moving expenses. Sue never contacted me again. Peggy chose to victimize me further by sending my parents the cruelest and most unfair letter asking for money and embellishing the extent of my party life. I had planned on borrowing the money from my parents and then working two summer jobs to pay them back. My mother, without consulting me, sent her a healthy sum of money, confirming that she too was less than pleased with me.

That was over 20 years ago, and I still fantasize from time to time about ways to get revenge if I ever run into her again."

Bev

Be realistic in expecting at least a few problems; even identical twins fight.

"I don't understand what happened. Jill and I were best friends and sorority sisters in college, but the minute we rented an apartment together after graduating, she turned into a vindictive wench. She thought she was too good to stick her hand down inside the toilet bowl to clean it or to be seen carrying out the garbage. Of course, we never had to do that in college."

Carol

"We get along great as long as Mitch's girlfriend isn't around. I can't stand her because she never shuts up. I try to like her but she gets mad because she'll be rambling on, and then she asks me a question, and I can't answer because I have no idea what she's blabbing about. Then the tears start and they're both mad at me."

Barney

Do not save your platform on moral issues until after you've moved in together.

"What an unpleasant turn of events when Sally announced that she would prefer I not keep beer for my boyfriend in her religious refrigerator!"

Kim

"I never dreamt Rob would so adamantly disapprove of my girlfriend spending the night. It ruined everything for me. She lives three hours away and I can't see spending money for a hotel room."

Joe

Choose someone whose feelings about smoking are parallel with your own.

It is highly unlikely that you will choose to live with a smoker if you are a non-smoker, but if you do, make sure you set limits. Will the smoker promise to step outside or restrict smoking to only one room?

If both of you are non-smokers, don't make the mistake of not discussing your expectations about smoking visitors. It has become fairly common for people to ask permission before lighting up, but you should be clear on this issue in case one of you would allow it and the other would rather not.

If you are both smokers, and one of you decides to quit, then you'll need to set new rules. There is no one as anti-smoking as an ex-smoker.

"I would go crazy looking for my cigarette lighter or a pack of matches, or I'd reach for the last cigarette in my purse and find that Leah had already smoked it. That's what finally made me decide it was time to quit. It was also the perfect excuse for moving out since I couldn't stand her anyway."

Tony

Hash over your views on drugs and alcohol with any new prospect.

"I thought Regina was just plain goofy, so prior to moving in together, I got a real kick out of her. Soon I discovered she was flipping out on anti-depressants, and illegally so. I began to feel like an outsider because most of her friends did drugs too, and when they were around, they whispered a lot, sensing my disapproval. I thought druggies were the ones who were supposed to feel paranoid. Instead, it was me."

Emily

"Most of my friends drink, but I don't because I have sugar diabetes. I never thought John's partying would be a problem, but he got drunk every weekend and puked all over the bathroom. I was forced to either clean it up or leave it until he sobered up and did it himself."

James

Consider the difference in your financial standing.

If you are jealous because your roommate is vacationing in the tropics, and you can only afford to soak your feet in a bucket on the back porch, your feelings are understandable. What is not understandable is why you would put yourself in that position to begin with.

The flip side would be living with someone who seems to be forever struggling financially, hem hawing around when the rent or bills are due. If you anticipate either situation, then you'd best avoid moving in together.

"It really wasn't Mark's fault that I resented him. His parents picked up the tab for everything. I had to work in the school cafeteria washing trays and mopping floors, and I had to study like crazy to maintain a meager scholarship. On top of that, I was accumulating a huge student loan that I'd have to start paying back as soon as I graduated. I never thought I'd ever get a break.

And it never failed. As soon as I would get back to the apartment from my job, dead tired, and having to study, he would be all decked out in his designer duds, ready to go out on the town."

James

Be wary of a temporary deal.

"My boss, Tom, was on the verge of proposing to his more than eager girlfriend, and planned on marrying her in six months or so. She was having trouble with her unemployed, trashy neighbors, who apparently slashed her tires after she complained to their landlord that they were keeping her up nights. So he wondered if she could live with me until the inevitable wedding. Two years have passed, and I'm going out of my skull trying to figure out how to get rid of her and not lose my job.

Tom now wants her to finish her bachelor's degree before he proposes, and she's dragging her feet thinking they'll get married so she won't *have* to finish. How am I ever going to get out of this mess?"

Ellen

Keep in mind the old cliché, *Birds of a Feather*, when choosing a roommate.

Shared interests are one sure-fire method for predicting compatibility. Opposites may attract in romantic relationships, but in platonic situations, the more alike you are, the better you are apt to get along.

"We're having a custody battle over the channel changer. My favorite time of the day is right after work when I can kick off my shoes and watch a talk show. Tracey is hooked on soaps and insists she watch three hours of taped shows the minute she comes home. She calls her friends to discuss plot developments, and has even missed work when things are about to get exciting. Good grief!"

Marissa

"I laughed when Bill told me he liked country music. That is the *only* type of music I have never listened to. After a few months of a daily dose of it, I'm not laughing anymore. I feel violated, the way my grandmother would feel sitting on the front row of a head banger concert."

Chad

Reveal to one another all your fanaticisms so there won't be any surprises.

"When I'm not clothed, I do not want anyone looking at me. No one is allowed in the bathroom while I'm in there, or in my bedroom while I'm dressing. Molly keeps telling me it isn't a big deal to be seen naked, but by golly, it is to me. Not everyone is a size 8 like her. If she doesn't lay off, I'm going to move out."

Brenda

"Because of my Neanderthal ex-husband, I cannot tolerate any hair in the bathroom that didn't fall off of my own body. As long as Jill cleans up her hair, she can get away with most anything else."

Francie

"I'd rather take a beating than miss watching Ally McBeal on Monday nights."

Nina

"As long as I don't have to listen to the details of anyone's sex life, I can live with anything. What goes on in your bedroom should be kept private."

Peggy

Don't take in strays thinking you'll somehow save them.

"I ran into an old friend at a class reunion who seemed down and out. I got the bright idea that I'd help her get a fresh start by offering her a place to stay until she could find a job and get back on her feet. The next morning, I immediately regretted what I'd done, knowing I'd had too much to drink, but I didn't really expect her to take me up on it. But she did, so I went through with the plan anyway, thinking that eventually it might be nice to be sharing living expenses.

After four months, she's doing great, but still hasn't offered to pay a cent towards anything. She keeps skirting the issue by mentioning how she needs a more reliable car and a better wardrobe so she can find a better job. The funny thing is, my car isn't as nice as the one she's driving, and she's using up more closet space than I am!"

Pam

"I found out I wasn't the full-blown philanthropist I thought I was after I took in a recently divorced friend. When she wasn't eating all of my food, or running up my phone bill talking to her kids, she was laying around crying all the time, depressing the heck out of me. Eventually she moved out. From now on, I'll just stick to saving the whales or something."

Hallie

Don't live with someone you work with.

"This was the dumbest thing I ever did. You can't imagine the grief I got when I got a promotion and Robert didn't. I became his supervisor!"

Ted

"My parents were in hog heaven the year I lived with a co-worker because I visited them every weekend just to get away from her. I thought I'd go bananas working side-by-side and living together. Even married couples don't spend that much time together."

Donna

"Can you imagine what it was like when we began to fall out and Carrie started airing our dirty laundry at work? She ruined my reputation with her lies and eventually I had to quit."

Olivia

Don't believe it when a prospect tells you: *This would be a great situation for you because I'll never be around. I practically live with my lover.*

If you are counting on total privacy or help with the bills in a situation like this, stop fantasizing. Reality will never meet the expectation.

"I was a fool when I believed my "phantom" roommate was going to cough up half of the utility bills. The reason why I decided to share an apartment in the first place was to split everything: the rent *and* the utilities. He was never there, so I should have known he'd balk when I presented him with a list of his share of the first month's bills."

Ryan

"Connie was true to her word. For an entire semester, she spent every night with her boyfriend and kept a few clothes around to fool her parents. The bad part? When she stopped by now and then, she would scare the beejeebers out of me busting through the door, especially at night."

Joni

"At first it was a fabulous arrangement because I crave privacy, yet I can't afford a place of my own. Then it became a nightmare because Beth and her boyfriend split up. Not only did I suddenly have a full-time roommate, I had a full-time sniveling, whining roommate."

Darlene

Be upfront if you expect to have a regular parade of guests.

Do you have nieces and nephews who will be coming by now and then to watch a little Disney? Will you be cooking dinner for your eighty year-old grandmother every Sunday, or will you continue the ritual of tapping a keg for your buddies during Monday Night Football?

"Kirby's retired father stops by on Sunday mornings for coffee. If my girlfriend has spent the night, she just about pees her pants waiting for him to leave before she comes out of my bedroom."

Joe

"Even though Sue was 13 years younger than me, she seemed so mature and responsible, I just *knew* we would get along. It was her friends that I had never considered. They were still at that stage where they were through college, but not past the stage of smashing beer cans on their heads and playing the stereo at full tilt — and she thought it was funny.

The brouhaha that ensued after the bars had closed and they converged on our apartment was unreal. Some of my older friends helped me squelch that little routine by simply stopping by when I knew they'd be coming. After one look at that older crowd, the place cleared out real fast, and they never came back."

Mercedes

Don't move away from home until you are ready for the responsibilities that come with it.

"Derek and I couldn't wait to get our own place and be free of our parents. We were both able to do whatever we wanted, whenever we wanted. Then our buddies, who still lived at home, started camping out in our apartment, drinking and wrecking the place. When we noticed the town cops were constantly driving by our place, we got scared, bailed out, and moved back home."

Beau

Don't move in with a "downer".

"I'd come home from work and Tom would spill his guts about how awful his whole day had been and who died and who all had lost their jobs and anything but good news. It depressed me so badly I had to start going to the gym straight from work or I couldn't get off of the couch because I felt horrible."

Dan

"A mutual friend of ours was killed in a car accident, so Bobbie and I rode to the funeral home together. On the way home, I commented on the nice way the embalmers had tilted her head so that you could see her face better. That was the only comforting thing I could find about the whole ordeal, but *Miss Doom and Gloom*, as I call her, had to shoot that thought down too. She told me her neck and been broken and that was why her head was turned funny. I used to be a pretty happy person until I moved in with her."

Stel

"George thought he was Nostradamus reincarnated, able to predict far in advance where my actions would lead. If I had one beer, I was sure to total my car, killing someone in the process, or if I didn't immediately return my parents' calls, they would probably cut me out of their will. What a strange bird he was."

Ned

Avoid those with the tendency to be insanely jealous.

"When I started working on a bachelor's degree at night to get out of the rut of a low paying secretarial job, Cindy became so envious she tried to undermine my efforts. I should have known this would be her reaction. She was jealous of every other girl when we were in high school, so I guess it was my turn.

On the nights I didn't have class, I religiously retreated to my bedroom to study. If she wasn't turning up the volume on the stereo to a ridiculous level, she was laughing like a hyena at some stupid TV show. Who laughs out loud when they're alone anyway?

After a year of being miserable, I moved in with someone else, and I haven't seen her since."

Allie

When moving in with more than one person, don't expect the harmonious lifestyle of the Brady Bunch.

"The rent is cheap, but I have to share a bedroom and make plans a week in advance to go to the bathroom."

Teddie

"Renting a house with seven other girls sounded like a fabulous idea because I thought it would insure that I would always have a rich, fulfilling social life. I was never lonely, but it also meant that I wouldn't ever be able to relax in the tub, cook an entire meal alone in the kitchen, get a good night's sleep, or watch whatever I wanted on television."

Sami

"Six guys in my dorm got together and rented a house our senior year. It was spooky because there would be people hanging around the house that you didn't even know. Sure enough, we got ripped off because two guys walked in off the street. I even spoke to them as they were coming down the stairs after they had emptied my wallet!"

Jeff

"To make it financially when I got my first job, I had to share an apartment with three other girls. Little by little, we discovered our personal belongings were coming up missing. The thief among us was just too clever — she complained about her things disappearing more than we did!

When the leather coat my parents had bought me for Christmas had obviously been stolen, I was distraught beyond words. Months later, the culprit's little sister showed up on our doorstep wearing my coat! Luckily, her stupidity solved the mystery."

Stacey

If you're adventurous or desperate enough to consult the want-ads, meet in a safe place, be clear about what you're looking for, and ask for references.

"We met at a coffee shop and she said I was quite a *biscuit*. I knew right then and there that she was gay. Had she disclosed this information outright, it wouldn't have been a problem for me. I might have even introduced her to a couple of my lesbian friends. But hitting on me was so tacky, I ended the meeting and continued my search elsewhere."

Cammie

"After serving eight years for vehicular homicide, I thought I would never be able to put my life back together again. I moved across the country, rather than face the family and friends of the girl I had killed. The accident was totally my fault having been drunk, and I don't even remember the crash. Worst of all, I was in love with her.

At first I thought I could just forget about it and escape the memories, but I was wrong. When I filled out my first job application, there it was: *Any convictions?* Shocked back to reality, I decided to be honest and up-front while looking for employment and someone to share living expenses with. Subsequently, I found both within a couple of weeks.

I've lived with Scott for a couple of years, and he's never mentioned the accident since the day I answered his ad. All he asked was, *Are you sorry?"*

Ned

Don't move in with anyone your "ex" can use against you to take away visitation rights with your kids.

"Pete was a widower, and needed help with the rent to raise his teenage son. The first time my daughter came to visit, I knew I'd made a huge mistake. His kid was obviously lusting after her, and it looked like the feeling might be mutual. I didn't sleep all weekend, afraid he'd sneak into her bedroom.

My ex-wife gave me all kinds of grief even though I cancelled her visits until I found another place to live."

Tyler

Don't live with a habitual loser believing that with your guidance, you'll be able to turn his or her life around.

Unless you're an expert at changing self-defeating behavior in others, this arrangement will get old real fast.

"Stan was 26 years old and still an undergraduate majoring in art. That should have told me enough to know he was headed for Loserville. I tried to help him out anyway by posing for hours for a portrait for a painting class he was taking. Hopefully, he would get an A and I would get a fabulous gift for my parents for Christmas. Instead, he dropped the course believing he could free lance, and asked me to pay him $500 for the portrait, which was hideous. I looked like Porky Pig with a perm."

James

"Talk about guilt. I thought I could transform Kara from a painfully shy girl, into a confident, sophisticated woman. She would be sort of a secret little project for me and wouldn't I be quite the hero!

Instead, she completely ignored my advice. She was happy with who she was — a complete and utter bore — and resented that I thought she needed to change."

Miranda

"I was concerned and supportive of Ralph's job hopping until I figured out he was just taking financial advantage of me and not really trying. The bottom line was that he just didn't want to go to work every day. And, he didn't want to work his way up. He thought he should be able to demand a higher salary when he'd only worked somewhere a few weeks."

Paul

Don't discount relatives as roommates. It can be easier to establish and enforce rules having unconditional love to back you up.

"After my divorce, I moved in with my younger sister who was spoiled rotten as a child. The first thing she told me when I started to clean the place up was that there was some kind of *sticky tar* on top of her refrigerator, so I shouldn't bother trying to clean up there. That *tar* was from years of her not wiping up the dust, which I promptly pointed out to her. From then on, I made it clear what I expected her do and she did it."

Gena

"My brother is the only person I've ever lived with that I feel totally comfortable expressing exactly how I feel. Why didn't I think of sharing an apartment with him years ago?"

Kim

Look out for *hidden agendas*.

"Nancy viewed our apartment as merely a pit-stop until she could nab a husband. There were boxes and boxes of household items stacked everywhere that she was saving, just like her virginity, for married life. She bought a pricey recliner for Mr. Perfect, even though she has yet to meet him, and filled it with dolls so no one would sit in it and wear it out. She even used my bath towels so hers would stay nice.

Ironically, as soon as I had completely furnished and decorated the apartment myself, I met someone. I was the one who ended up marrying first, and I wasn't even looking."

Renea

"The phone never stops ringing, and the traffic in and out of our front door is driving me mad. Always looking for a way to make an extra buck, Joe has started a home-based business selling T-shirts and sporting equipment to local coaches. I feel like I'm living in a locker room at tournament time."

Ned

Don't count on a cozy arrangement, but complete lunacy, if you move in with your boyfriend's roommate's girlfriend, or vice versa.

"Debbie and I knew each other fairly well because our boyfriends lived together and we had spent a lot of time at their apartment. When we simultaneously found ourselves looking for a new place to live, it seemed logical that we should find a place together, and the guys cheered us on. What seemed like a cute idea quickly turned into an irksome entanglement of our lives.

Debbie and Roger were homebodies, and extremely lazy. Mark and I were workaholics and frequently went out in the evenings to decompress. The two of them became envious of our success at work and the money we had to go out, and began making snippy remarks, making us feel guilty for living. Their relationship had become stale and their lives boring from hanging around the apartment and watching ignorant sitcoms for entertainment.

They would trash one apartment, and while Mark and I were cleaning it up, they were trashing the other. The tension was increasing by the moment, and escalated as they were somehow making us feel responsible for their unhappiness.

We began synchronizing our quitting times at work so that on the way home, we could pass by the boys' place first, and if they were there, we would retreat to our place just to avoid them. Spending an evening apart was out of the question, because our singular presence was viewed as an intrusion on their pathetic lives.

One of the happiest days of my life was when they decided to get married. Mark and I waited several years before we tied the knot, because we wanted to recapture the normalcy and freedom we lost while living in that distressing situation."

Carmen

"I was never able to tell my boyfriend anything new or exciting. Abby would run over to the guys' apartment and blab everything before I could get there. Even if I asked her not to, she couldn't help herself. I still hate her guts."

Jo Ann

"After Fred and I broke up, Ellen told him everything I was doing. She claimed she had the right to do so because they were still friends. Give me a break! I had to sneak around to start dating again, because she kept inviting him over to try and get us back together again."

Cindy

Never participate in a fraudulent arrangement to fool the justice system or anyone else.

Putting all moral issues aside, you will most likely be the one to pay in the end.

"My nephew was using my address to avoid having to live in the dorm his freshman year. The college he attended required it, and he wanted to live in an apartment so he would have more freedom. Someone called to speak with him, and I gave out his phone number, unknowingly to someone in the financial aid office. He was caught, and the only way to avoid being dismissed was to move in with me for real. My life and my home were completely wrecked by an 18-year-old for three long months. When I laid down the law and demanded he help around the house, he decided living in a dorm wouldn't be so bad after all. The whole ordeal ruined my relationship with him and his parents."

Ashley

"I don't know what I was thinking when I agreed to pretend that my best friend was living with me when he was going through a messy divorce. Infidelity was one of the issues and I was helping him cover up the fact that he was shacking up with his secretary. His crazy wife started showing up all hours of the night pounding on the door and screaming obscenities, waking up the whole neighborhood. Then I had to miss three days of work because I was subpoenaed to court."

Sammie

If you are highly ambitious, be aware that living with a "do nothing" may get on your nerves.

"It totally amazes me how Tammy can have the nerve to ask me not to run the sweeper when she's watching TV. That's *all* she does, except for going to work, and I'll bet she doesn't do anything there either."

Jenna

"Every spare moment Rick has, he's horizontal on the couch. Other than going to work and stopping to pick up fast food on the way home, he has absolutely no life other than watching sports on TV.

He keeps telling me that I'm going to work my life away, but actually, I've been working more and more hoping to get a raise and get out of that apartment."

Zeb

Be wary of living with your lover if you're looking forward to marriage someday.

Are you *sure* this is what you want? If you're planning on marrying at a later date, do you realize statistics show that a sizeable number of couples who live together before tying the knot end up divorced or never even make it to the alter? Why?

My guess is, heeding warnings from seasoned mates, immature couples erroneously believe that once married, *things will get better*. So all you aspiring brides need to stop believing that the slob laying around your apartment will surely turn into the Prince of Never-Never-Land once you're married. And if you're a guy, I hate to break it to you, but your girl-friend will *not* want sex even more after you're married, and she won't start baking homemade bread to save you money either.

But if you've already set your mind to this arrangement, the good news is that couples who are just "playing house" usually behave quite well because one knows the other has the option to leave with few strings attached.

Consider this: If you haven't paid the security deposit or signed the lease, it's not too late to back out.

"Right before college graduation, I found out that Cindy had betrayed my confidence, and we were planning to rent an apartment together in the fall. She told my ex-boyfriend I'd had an abortion, and I couldn't even imagine living with her again after that.

I should have known, because she ripped apart everyone we knew in the privacy of our dorm room. Nothing was sacred to her; she told it all. So, I shouldn't have been blind to the fact that she was probably spilling her guts about me too.

I was lucky because I had a couple of months to stew about it before I realized that life's just too short. I wasn't going to honor our verbal commitment even though it would have only been for a year."

Tracey

"My boyfriend, Tom, and I looked at several apartments before we found one close enough to our jobs, and for the right price. Once we decided which one to take, some of the comments he had made during the search kept playing over and over again in my mind. *Are you sure you don't mind if we don't have a dishwasher? Here's a closet where you can keep your cleaning supplies. I hope you don't have any trouble finding curtains for that big window.*

My drab little apartment didn't seem so bad after all. At least I only have myself to take care of."

Trina

OBVIOUSLY YOU'VE MISTAKEN ME FOR YOUR MAID

(WHEN I WANT TO START TAKING CARE OF SOMEONE ELSE, I'LL PROCREATE, THANK YOU.)

When considering domestic responsibilities, people can be divided into basically two categories: those who hate to clean, and those who hate to clean but do it anyway. Of all the problems you will encounter, this is likely to be the subject that will come up most often, or it will create a smoldering atmosphere if not addressed.

The good news is that most housekeeping disputes can be viewed in black and white. It's either clean or dirty, you either made the mess or you didn't, and it's either your turn to perform the chore or it's not.

The exception will be those gray areas in which your standards differ. That is why you need to agree on a routine early, and stick to it.

Demand that chores be divided equally.

If you are not domestic by nature, then you need to ask what should be done and how often. If cleaning seems disproportionately important to this person, then you need to compromise while divvying up chores. Work up a schedule on paper if you need to, but make it flexible in that you are not expected to strictly adhere to cleaning on specified days of the week.

"Toni was of the erroneous opinion that because I was a teacher and had summers off, I should be her personal maid for three months a year. What really irked me was that I would put in 12 to 14 hour days during the school year, while she was still on her measly 40 hour per week schedule, and she did nothing to help me out."

Jeannie

"I do more by accident than Phil does on purpose."

Mike

Don't ignore the time frame. If you agree to complete a task every week, then do it every 7 days.

"Why did I get rid of Teri? I didn't like our lop-sided cleaning schedule. One week I would clean, and the next week she wouldn't."

Hazel

Fight the urge to compensate for a slowpoke or someone who can't match your blistering perfectionism. You'll end up doing the job yourself — permanently.

"Allie said she would make up for not helping out as soon as she had a free Saturday. Her grueling work schedule left her too tired to do anything during the week. I wised up to the fact that no one ever has a free Saturday, and I was getting stuck doing everything myself.

It only took a single seventy-five dollar therapy session to come to the realization of what was really going on. The counselor said, "Your devotion to your own obsessive, neurotic needs seems to be clouding your ability to recognize the truly important issues in life. Translation: Stop cleaning all the time and get a life.""

Rebecca

Don't be a brat and start doing your chores when you know you'll be annoying, thinking you'll get out of the responsibility.

"Ha! I knew if I ran the sweeper right after work when Beth wanted to watch Rosie O'Donnell, I knew she'd offer to do it for me later."

Sami

If you are a clean freak, be careful about upsetting the order of someone else's clutter.

"I never dreamt a guy could be so fastidious about housekeeping. Ned was invading my territory by cleaning up what I considered to be organized clutter. I know you can't win with these obsessive-compulsive types, so there was only one thing I could do: Confine my messes to my bedroom and keep the door shut."

Dustin

"I hated working evenings because I could be sure that Terri would take advantage of my time away to clean up what she considered to be an obscene mess. To me, that squalor was my desk, computer, books, and papers, all kept exactly where I wanted them. She rearranged everything, causing me a great deal of stress in making sense out of where I had last stopped working."

Melanie

If you don't really know how to clean, just ask.

"Geri was ignorant about keeping house — or at least she pretended to be. She swore that you never needed to mop the kitchen floor if you kept it swept regularly with just a broom. So, guess who got stuck mopping the floor.

In the dead of winter, and at the height of my resentment, I stopped taking the throw rugs outside to shake when I mopped. I went into her bedroom and shook those rugs until I thought my arms would come out of the sockets. Her room was so filthy, she was none the wiser, and it sure made me feel better."

Julianna

"Erica was a nurse and a psycho about germs, but I went ballistic when I caught her scrubbing the top of my antique farm table with bleach!"

Darcy

"Jon's mother didn't teach him anything. I assumed she had waited on him hand and foot, but I learned quite the opposite when I went home with him one weekend. His mother's house was so foul, at any moment I expected Uncle Fester to walk through the door."

Charles

Don't expect to be excused just because you're clueless. Even the totally inept can fool the fussiest of housekeepers by following this simple plan:

In the kitchen:
Start with a bucket of suds (use a no-rinse cleaning solution), and work from the top down. Wipe down all counter tops, backsplashes, stovetop and door, range hood, refrigerator top and door, sticky cabinet fronts, tabletop and chairs, and any appliances that are frequently used. Use glass cleaner on any interior windows. Mop the floor, and you're done.

Bathroom:
Again, start with a bucket of no rinse suds. Wipe everything down starting at the top. Don't use anything but glass cleaner, rubbing alcohol, or diluted vinegar on mirrors or you'll ruin them. Keep a bleaching tablet especially made to clean toilets, in the tank, and then you can get away with not sticking your hand in the bowl.

Don't forget to shake the rugs *outside*. If heavily soiled, most can be thrown in the washer, but hang them up to dry. You can also machine wash soap scum and mildew off of shower curtains. Throw in a towel to provide the scrubbing action.

Wait until you're ready to shower to wipe down the shower stall. Then you can do it naked and use the showerhead to rinse without soaking your clothes.

Living room, office, etc.:

Use glass cleaner on the TV screen, interior windows, and any other glass surfaces. Do this first so you won't have furniture polish on your hands. Spray the furniture polish on a rag, not the furniture, and run it over any wood. Use an electro-statically charged dry cloth on surfaces you're not sure about such as VCR's and books.

Hopefully you have a vacuum cleaner that has a great filter and a dusting attachment. The new ones will suck up anything and everything, so don't run yours over throw rugs, and be careful not to suck up the cord. Take throw rugs outside and shake them. Use the dusting attachment to run over upholstery, and to reach where the machine won't go.

Bedroom:

If this is where you're hiding all your clutter, keep the door closed. Apply the same rules for cleaning except you need to wash your sheets before you start or you'll stir up a new dust bowl.

Read the directions on cleaning products before you ruin something.

"The dust cover on my stereo is completely ruined because Jody sprayed furniture polish on it."

Marsha

"Take it from me, you'll ruin the finish on a fiberglass tub if you use abrasive cleansers."

Fred

When the garbage can is full, tie the bag shut, replace it with a new bag, and take the garbage out, period.

"Everywhere I've lived, I've always been the one stuck taking out the trash. Sure, I've tried playing the game *let's-see-how-high-they-will-pile-the-garbage-before-they-take-it-out*, but trust me, it never works. Everyone shoves more and more trash down in the can until the sides are deformed and it's wedged in so you can't get the bag out. Or, they balance stuff on top so that if you put one more thing on top of the pile, everything comes spilling out all over the floor."

Mike

"Our trash bin is inside a closet and Ashley doesn't even look when she throws something inside. You open the door and an avalanche comes rolling out onto your feet. And if I don't replace the bag immediately, she'll throw slop inside without one, and then I have to wipe out the container or there will be goop all over the outside of the bag. Yuck!"

Nell

"Bo's response to my request to start taking out the garbage was to not use the can at all. He started sitting grocery sacks all over the kitchen floor and filled them up one by one. They were leaking all over the linoleum and there were food stains streaking the walls from flinging garbage across the room. I finally came unglued and volunteered to take out the trash if he would just start using the can again."

Mary Sue

Wipe your feet at the doorway.

"I hate it in the winter when Carly tramps all over the apartment in her snow covered boots and I get my socks wet."

Penny

"When you can tell I've just cleaned, Jeff is afraid to get the door mat dirty, so he steps over it onto the carpet. Duh."

Van

Flush the toilet every time you use it.

"Need this be said? Jenny thinks if she just *pees a bit*, she doesn't need to. Then, there's always yellow, smelly scum buildup in the bowl."

Denise

Wipe the toilet seat off when your aim is off.

"I hate it when I burst into the bathroom and the seat is soiled and it is too late to clean it off before I have to sit on it."

Robbie

"Barbie is on a liquid diet. I could just croak when I have to go in that bathroom. Her lack of solid food gives her a constant case of explosive diarrhea which ends up all over the back of the toilet seat."

Heather

If you empty the toilet paper roll, replace it!

"I made up this game, *Let's see if I can make Jamie change the empty roll*, but I never win. After a few days of refusing to change it myself, it becomes quite amusing. I swear she has to be licking her fingers. I lasted a whole week once, meticulously sneaking wads of tissue into the bathroom, before she finally broke down and sat a roll on the back of the toilet. For me, that was a real break through, even though she didn't put it in the holder."

Sherri

Put the toilet seat down when finished.

Wanda

Put the toilet seat back up!

Wanda's Boyfriend

Rinse your gargle and gaggle out of the bathroom sink.

"It doesn't matter to me if Cindy ever cleans the bathroom, but the one thing I can't tolerate is the slime she leaves behind after she brushes and gargles."

Amanda

Put your toys away.

"You need a bulldozer to find the couch in our living room. Suzie never puts anything away. Just once I'd like to be able to sit down without having to clear away a pile of CD's and magazines, or having a needle stuck up my rump from one of her half-finished craft projects."

Tammie

Wash your own dirty dishes, even if you only have a few.

"It never fails, when I start to wash my dishes, Sue comes galloping into the kitchen and dumps her stuff down into the dishwater. Who does she think I am, Cinderella? Obviously, she thinks I don't mind, because she only has a few things, but gee whiz, all the time? Give me a break. She could wash them when I'm finished with mine, but even if I leave them, she doesn't take the hint and just leaves them for the next day."

Pinky

"Ben can cook better than my grandmother, and I love it. What I don't love is cleaning up the mess. I demanded that we take turns washing dishes, so he went out and blew money on paper plates and plastic cups for when it's *his* turn. And he expects us to get married someday?"

Korri

"I get sick and tired of having to move Jenny's dirty dishes around just to find the kitchen sink so I can fix myself something to eat. I've even tried filling the sink with sudsy water and throwing her dishes in it. She just let the water out and piled them back on the counter top!"

Liz

Don't leave greasy pans on the stove thinking you'll reuse them.

"Eric must have a cast iron stomach. He fries hamburgers every night for supper in the same skillet. He never gets sick, but I do just from smelling and looking at the built up grease.

We stopped by his mother's one evening, and she offered to feed us supper. I couldn't believe my eyes when she walked over to the stove and turned the burners on underneath what looked to be petrified chili to me. Apparently they eat like that all the time."

Mitch

Clean up splattered grease, not only from the stove, but from the exhaust hood too.

"When I clean up the kitchen, I end up having to clean up Terri's greasy messes too. Can't she see that gunk?"

Torri

Clean up spills in the bottom of the oven.

"If you bake something that might run over, all you have to do is put a cookie sheet underneath the dish. Jason finally learned after he caught the oven on fire. He must have slept though grade school, because even my eight-year-old sister knows to throw flour on a kitchen fire, not water."

Jeremy

When cooking on top of the stove, don't let food boil over onto the burners. Either use a bigger pot or lower the heat.

"We have gunk all over the burners and down inside the stove that smokes and smells up the apartment. This has become a small-scale war in which I sneak into the kitchen and turn the flame down when Amanda is cooking, and then she marches in and turns it right back up. One of the burners has even stopped working, which is a real hindrance to her since her only method of cooking is to boil the snot out of everything."

Missy

Cover food in the microwave with cellophane, a paper towel, or a microwave-safe lid before nuking.

"Any idiot should be able to operate a microwave. If you happen to live with one that doesn't, microwave a cup of water to loosen the splatters. That's what I have to do because Sara, who by the way has a B.S. degree in chemistry, still manages to clog up the protective grill by not covering things, or she'll set the timer for far too long and her dinner will explode all over the place."

Josey

If you are causing a stench, then don't *cover* it up, *clean* it up.

"The worst thing about body odor is that people usually cannot smell themselves. Ron is one of the cleanest people I know, but he wears the same workout gear over and over again to cut down on laundry. Gag me!"

Chris

"For the longest time, Jan had an unidentifiable, pungent smell in her bedroom. I had to shut the door just to sit in the living room because it was so strong. I think she must have smelled it too, because she ran a fan night and day in there, even when she wasn't home.

I discovered the culprit by accident, the first time I went to a tanning salon. When I came out, my skin smelled like her bedroom! She went twice a week and then slept on the same sheets for a month or longer. She was basically a gross person anyway, so I just moved out."

Teresa

Volunteer for chores that you don't mind doing or whatever you are best at.

"I didn't mind putting on my headphones and running the sweeper all over the place. In fact, I do it almost every other night and it really cuts down on having to dust."

Marilee

"My job was to keep the kitchen clean. Connie would have crapped if she knew how I mopped the floor though. I put on old socks, slopped a little water and cleaner down, and then slid all over the floor. Then I took a bath towel and sopped up the water. It made me laugh doing it that way because she was such an immaculate housekeeper. Of course I've grown up a little since then."

Jodie

"We have a dungeon-type basement and I'm terrified of bugs, so Denise does all the laundry so I won't have to go down there. I keep up with the rest of the place so she won't slack off on keeping my things washed."

Terri

When asked to clean up a mess you've made, do it immediately.

"My fiancée was coming for dinner, so I rushed home from work, expecting as always, to have to clean up the kitchen from Patsy's mess the night before. Even though I told her Ron was coming over for dinner and asked that she please clean up after herself, I never dreamed she would break down and actually do it. To my surprise, the kitchen was spotless!

I flipped the oven on to preheat and ran to undress to shower before cooking dinner. A smokey odor began to pour out of the oven, thank goodness, *before* I got into the shower. She had hidden her dirty dishes in the oven and the pot handles were melting!"

Kylie

"I knew Karen had a lot of friends and would be entertaining frequently, so I said truthfully from day one that I wouldn't mind. I just asked that she clean up after them. The trouble was, she would wait for a couple of days before picking up even one empty beer bottle or pizza box, so I usually ended up doing it all for her.

I starting getting mad and kicking things out of the way just so I could find a place to sit down. She interpreted this to mean that I didn't want her to have anyone over at all, but that's not what I meant. I just wanted her to clean up the mess.

Now that the problem is out in the open, she knows it's her choice. If she's going to ask people over, she's going to clean up after them as soon as they leave."

Jessie

You can keep peace as a clutterbug if you simply confine your belonging to your bedroom and keep the door shut.

Those who leave a trail wherever they go are bound to drive people who are fastidiously neat bonkers. This issue is not to be confused with your lack of dusting, sweeping, mopping, and other general cleaning. It involves only one thing: clutter.

If you have a case of the dropsies, try curtailing the damage by not setting anything down, when you return home, until you are inside your bedroom. Then, start dropping and piling your belongings to your heart's content. And don't be offended when someone else shuts your door to block the view.

Clean the bathtub.

(Looks like the jury is still out on how often.)

"Sheila thinks I should scrub out the tub, even though I only take showers. Who has time to take a bath anyway? The minute I come out of the bathroom, she runs in like Attila the Hun, and does it herself, belly-aching the whole time. I say, if she has time to soak in the tub, she can clean it out herself!"

Sami

"There is something about standing in a shower stall full of somebody else's hair that makes me want to upchuck. Dave sheds like a Saint Bernard and never cleans up after himself. I'm not kidding. You could stuff a pillow with the hair he sheds."

Matt

Wipe up your hairspray residue and other annoying messes.

"Have you ever tried to get up from the toilet and the seat lifts up with you, glued to your haunches? Have you ever stepped out of the shower and felt your feet sticking to the floor and subsequently walked around all day with that tacky feeling inside your shoes? Have you ever stuck your toothbrush in your mouth and found that it tasted like lacquer? If you can relate, then you must live with a giant hairball like I do. She teases, picks, and sprays her hair until it becomes twice the size of her head. Then, she shellacs the finished product.

I don't expect the bathroom to be thoroughly mopped everyday, I just wish she would wipe up that gummy residue!"

Carol

"Cindy can bake like nobody's mother, but I wish she'd clean up a little better when she's through. To my horror, I arrived at work ready for a huge meeting, unaware of the white splotches down the side of my black suit. I had set my purse down on the kitchen counter that morning, and then threw the strap over my shoulder, not realizing that the bottom was covered with flour."

Ally

Make sure you rinse dishes thoroughly in hot water.

"I kept getting diarrhea until I figured out Joe wasn't completely rinsing the soap off of the dishes."

Jay

Keep dish cloths separate from other cleaning cloths.

"I caught Heather throwing the same foul rag she had just cleaned the toilet with into the kitchen sink!"

Sue

Don't run with the vacuum cleaner as if you're in the Kentucky Derby, and change the bag when it is full.

"The first time I ran the sweeper after I moved in with Cheri, the carpet was so dirty it sounded like I was vacuuming a gravel driveway. Then she got upset thinking I'd broken her machine because the bag exploded. She purchased it two years earlier and had never changed the bag."

Tracey

Don't lay newspapers where the print will rub off.

"You can see the exact spot on the couch where Donnie has laid the newspaper everyday since we moved in together."

Ike

Don't put your shoes on the furniture.

Now I know what my mom was yelling about when I was a kid. Oscar lays on the couch with his dirty tennis shoes on all the time. You can't sit on that end of the couch because it's so filthy the dirt rubs off on the back of your pants."

Tim

Stay off of the furniture when you are dripping wet with sweat.

"Our upholstery stinks. I would shampoo it, but what's the use? Adam spends evenings working out, and then plops down on the couch in his sweaty gym clothes. I'm no cream puff, but there is a limit to how much filth I can put up with."

Dean

Don't use the back of chairs as coat hangers.

"All of our kitchen chairs are draped with coats because everyone is too lazy to hang them up. I bought a hall tree and put it right inside the door, but of course everyone just ignores it. They would have to actually lift their arms up to hang a coat on it and that would mean exerting far too much energy."

Rita

Don't make unnecessary messes in the first place.

"The imbecile I lived with was on a diet and made giant bowls of sugar-free gelatin, and slammed the refrigerator door shut so hard it would slosh over the sides of the bowl and drip off of whatever was on the shelves below. After she moved out, I tried to pull out all the drawers and shelves to clean, and the bottom drawer wouldn't budge. There was a two-inch sheet of goo molding it to the bottom of the fridge."

Sherry

"Jackie apologizes over and over again for not ever having the time to help me clean, and then what does she do? She buys a dog so big you could put a saddle on it and ride it around the apartment!"

Toni

"If I wanted to clean up after people, I would have gotten married and had 10 kids. Instead, I get to live with a slob who invites her inconsiderate friends over every weekend, leaving a trail of garbage behind when they leave. Why don't they take turns going to each other's places?"

Marsha

If you consistently have a problem sharing responsibilities, admit your shortcomings, and find a way to make up for it.

You don't mean to let things go, but you just can't help yourself. By the time you're good and ready to clean up, someone else has already unwillingly done it. How can you make up for not carrying your share of the load?

"Parry would do anything for me, except clean. He picks up groceries, brings in the mail, stops to buy a newspaper, cleans the snow and ice off of my car, returns movies and books for me, runs to the dry cleaners, and always takes out the garbage. You name it, he does it, so I don't mind doing most of the other chores."

Kelly

"Ken insists on paying more rent. Who can argue with that kind of guilt?"

Herb

"I find it strange that Karen will change the oil in my car, but she wouldn't be caught dead scrubbing out the toilet. It's like having a handyman around, so who needs to get married?"

Deanna

If you think no one really minds that you're not doing any chores, you'd better get some therapy.

"One Saturday, as usual, I cleaned the apartment from top to bottom while Sally tiptoed around me, polishing her nails, giving herself a facial, and performing other beauty rituals that took the entire day before her date with Bill. When he arrived, he commented on how wonderful everything looked and smelled. Not Sally, but the apartment.

I was in my bedroom peeling off my sweaty clothes when I heard her take credit for it all. Things were exactly the way she wanted them to appear — a beautiful girl who also had domestic skills. Woo-woo, had he hit the dating jackpot or what?

Of course the poor sap married her and now she boo-hoos because he expects her to take care of their house and she just can't keep up with it."

Bethany

"I lived with an inconsiderate cretin who announced that her hypercritical mother was coming to visit and she wanted our place to look spotless. This request was coming from someone who never lifted a finger during the year we had lived together. She wouldn't even wash her own dishes.

A week before the royal visit, I made it known that my efforts were about to come to a screeching halt. It made me giddy making up excuses for not having time to clean, and I emphasized that she shouldn't mind since I had been cleaning up after her for so long.

She tried her best to pick up the slack for once, but she just couldn't cut it. And when she tried to blame the shape of things on me, it just didn't fly. I can still hear her mother shouting, *I didn't raise you like this!*"

Kelly

If you can't help being a slob, ask what your greatest offense is, and work on that.

"I put a laundry basket in the bottom of my bedroom closet and gave Coryn permission to throw anything I left laying around into it."

Suzie

"Newspapers and dirty dishes! That's what drove everyone bonkers about me. I was the first one out the door in the morning, so I gave myself 15 extra minutes to take care of cleaning up these two things."

Sandra

"Janet called me a *glamour puss* because I completely covered the bathroom counter top with makeup and toiletries. I bought a gorgeous basket and started throwing everything in it."

Danielle

"Before I go to bed, I walk through every room I've destroyed and put everything back. This is actually starting to cure me of my topsy-turviness. I'm getting so I will think to put things away immediately so I won't accumulate so much stuff to pick up when I'm dog tired."

Betsy

"My live-in, Christine, demanded that I take my turn cleaning every other week. I just can't do it. I detest even the thought of it and I don't have time, so I now I pay my teenage sister to come over after school once a week and do it for both of us. If I would have known how much it was going to improve our relationship, I would have made this arrangement a long time ago."

Larry

If you are the lone clean freak living amongst a gang of real dirt balls, don't think that stopping your "free maid service" will turn the situation around.

If you stop cleaning in protest of having to do it all, you will soon find out that you have been busting your hump for no one but yourself. You hope someone else will finally become as appalled as you do when the swill becomes overwhelming, and they will dig right in. Yeah, right.

You will only end up seething at the chaos, while everyone else is totally oblivious to it. For them, it merely means having to step over or around a little extra disarray while you're off duty. No big deal.

"Even though our apartment was becoming an obstacle course, it didn't bother me in the least that Jessica was on a housekeeping strike. Of course my indifference made her madder than ever, but who cares if you can't see yourself in every mirrored surface? At least I started putting things away as I tripped over them. Shoot, I thought she actually enjoyed cleaning."

Neil

If you've been accused of setting your domestic standards too high, solicit the opinion of a trusted outsider.

"On the return trip from a glorious week-long vacation with my boyfriend, Adam, he became exasperated with me for fretting over what I anticipated my apartment to look like when we arrived home. My roommate with a filthy swine, and he was tired of hearing about it. He challenged that it could never be as bad as I let on. I bet that it could and would be. There would be no wager, just the satisfaction I would feel after proving my point.

We pulled into the parking lot and simultaneously burst into a fit of laughter. The curtains in the living room were dangling at an odd angle and there was trash sitting on the windowsill. This was a sure indicator of my victory.

As we breezed in through the doorway, I realized Adam was truly a good loser as he exclaimed kiddingly to my dumbfounded roommate, *What happened? Did you get robbed?* That couldn't have been the case because burglars wouldn't have left that big of a mess!"

Terri

COULD YOU BE ANY MORE ANNOYING?

(OH DEAR, I HOPE YOU'RE NOT TALKING ABOUT ME.)

Sometimes major disturbances are easier to deal with than continuous, annoying behavior. When we are clearly fighting an all-out battle, at least we can be self-assured in expecting sympathy, support, and advice from friends and family. But when faced with the small stuff that can just as easily drive you over the wall, it can be a lonely fight. You feel ridiculous complaining about irksome behavior when even your mother would say the same thing you would hear from a full-blown therapist: *Don't be such a wimp — assert yourself!*

It's just not that easy when you fear being pegged a chronic complainer without coping skills. Yet it can be infuriating wondering why these simple courtesies were not learned at the onset of puberty, or if they were, why they are not being extended to you.

Don't hog the bathroom.

"The very first morning after Sherri moved in, I got up to take a shower before going to work and found scads of wet clothing hanging from the shower rod. By the time I found somewhere to hang everything, I knew I'd be late for work. I thought, *Oh no, here we go.*

Sure enough, a few days later, I got up and found her sweaters soaking in the tub. I was so mad, I pulled the plug and shoved them to the back, took a shower anyway, and then left the mess. She was ticked off, but she didn't do it again."

Barb

"The girls at work get the biggest kick out of the fact that one of my desk drawers is filled with toothpaste, hairspray, and what-not. I have to go to work early just to finish getting ready because the prima donna I live with spends an eternity in our bathroom."

Brandy

"The gas station attendants at the corner all know me by name and snicker when they seem me coming. They know I'm just coming in to use the bathroom because ours in always in use."

Carmen

Don't use up all the hot water if you know there's a line for the shower.

"Every morning, Jodie washes a pile of dishes and then takes a long shower right before I get up for work. She could wash those stupid dishes some other time!"

Karen

"I spend most weekends out of town with relatives, but I drive home on Sunday mornings to get ready for church. My irascible roommate uses my car as her alarm clock! The minute I pull into my parking space, I can see her bedroom light flick on, and by the time I get inside, she is already in the shower. It doesn't matter what time I get there, she still does it, and then I have to hurry and take a cold shower to boot!"

Kendra

Don't change the TV station just because someone has left the room to use the bathroom or grab a snack.

"Talk about rude. If I knew the name of good reform school for channel surfers, I'd send Katie there."

Nancy

Don't cut up newspapers or magazines until everyone has read them.

"Did you ever start reading a really good article and then discover that some nincompoop has cut out a coupon on the back of one of the pages?"

Lois

Don't drink from the milk carton or put the empty carton back in the fridge.

"How barbaric can you get? I can see Barb's lipstick marks on the opening!"

Andrea

Treat your roommate's property with respect.

"I had pretty decent furniture until Sheila moved in. She gobbles down her dinner every night in front of the television, leaving water rings on my end tables and slopping food all over my upholstery. One day I noticed a cushion lying upside-down on the couch. I flipped it over the right way and discovered she had turned it over to try and hide a huge pizza colored stain.

She refuses to pay to have the couch recovered, so in revenge, I poured soda in her VCR. She can't prove I did anything to it, but now she's mad and moving out, which is exactly what I want too."

Robin

Don't let perishable food rot in the refrigerator taking up space.

"It burns me up to come home from the grocery store and there's no space for my food, and the fridge stinks because Billie is too lazy to throw anything out. Then I have to empty putrid smelling containers, wash the dishes, and take out the garbage or the whole apartment smells."

Shellie

Don't take a steamy shower right when a female roommate is trying to curl her hair.

"Not everyone is born with blow-dryable hair, so don't ruin what little we can accomplish with a curling iron."

Tammy

Don't block the driveway.

"Every once in awhile, Tommy will make me late for work because he's too lazy to park where there's room, just because he'd have to walk just a few extra steps. Then he gets mad when I have to wake him up if I can't find his keys."

Pat

You should have learned to share in kindergarten, and that now that you're grown up, that includes computer time.

"You'd think that since I was gracious enough to let Brooke use my computer, she'd let me on it once in awhile. She rushes home from work to beat me to it, and only to satisfy her latest addiction: playing Free Cell. I've worked out a schedule so I won't have to fight with her, but she keeps saying, *Just let me finish this game.*"

Joni

Computers are expensive toys. Don't play with one unless the owner is willing to share.

"My computer is the only thing I'm territorial about. I have files from work on it, and I don't want anyone reading my e-mail. I just happened to check the history file, looking for a web site I'd been in the night before, and discovered someone had been screwing around on the Internet. I reiterated to the three guys I live with that under no circumstances were they to use it *ever*.

I turned it off when I went on vacation, but when I returned, the message that the system had been improperly shut down flashed across the screen. So worse yet, whoever was playing around was clueless about computers. Then I thought, *Duh, why not just put a pass word on it?*"

Tom

Stick to a regular bathroom schedule on workdays, or stay out of the way!

Accidentally making someone late for a social engagement is forgivable, but constantly playing havoc with someone's livelihood is another story. Most people have enough trouble getting up in the morning and being on time without someone getting in the way. Stick to a regular bathroom schedule, and if you miss your turn, wait until the bathroom is free.

Wash your hands after you use the restroom.

"I'm a health teacher, so I'm a real stickler for hygiene. Arlene runs out of the bathroom and grabs the phone, the channel changer, kitchen utensils, or whatever, and it makes my skin crawl!"

Madeline

Use decent manners when eating.

"Rick would gag a maggot the way he eats. He never shuts up the entire time, so you not only get to view what he is chewing, you also get to wear what he spews across the table at you."

Charlie

"The good news is that I'm losing weight. That bad news is that I can no longer enjoy cooking or eating because Teresa grosses me out. She eats things like ice cream and cottage cheese right out of the carton, which I could probably protest and put a stop to. But, how do you tell someone they make you sick because they breathe heavily through their mouth while eating, when it's a result of chain smoking? That, I can't fix."

Carla

Only break wind in private.

"Sherry let one rip in the living room then ran into her bedroom to hide because my date was ringing the doorbell! I was mortified!"

Sara

Keep your fingers out of your nose.

"Even though Pete stops digging when I enter the room, I can see that he doesn't have a tissue. Where is he stashing it? I'm afraid to sit on the furniture!"

Carl

Don't be a noseblower in the shower.

"I could forgive the moron I live with if he would scrub out the tub, but anyone who does this could care less about hygiene."

Gena

Practice decent hygiene.

"If Alice isn't going to work, then she isn't going to shower or brush her teeth all day long. I usually have to find somewhere to go so I won't be subjected to the smell. What a scank."

Ronnie

Designate a specific spot to leave the mail every day.

"Sheri gets home from work before I do and picks up the mail, which I appreciate, but half the time, I can't find it. Sometimes she throws it on the kitchen table, and the rest of the time I have to search the apartment for it. My tax refund check laid in a pile on her bedroom floor and she almost threw it away with a stack of newspapers. I can't help but wonder if anything important has ever come and she didn't give it to me."

Jennifer

"I used to pick up the mail on my way out in the evenings and would throw it in the back seat of my car. Then, Trent freaked out and broke a window out of my car to get it. Why didn't he just say something? I didn't know he was waiting for a letter from some girl he'd met on vacation."

Hal

Respect your roommate's desire for sleep.

Just because you're awake doesn't mean everyone else wants to be awake too. If you're a night owl, fine. Stay up all night if you want to — it's a free country. Just let the rest of us sleep.

Don't keep hitting the snooze button on your alarm clock.

Keep the volume down on the TV, computer, stereo, etc.

Don't run the vacuum cleaner, garbage disposal, or any other cute little noisemakers.

Don't call your friends and say, "Call me back."

Don't slam doors or drawers.

Don't do your step aerobics unless you weigh less than 98 pounds.

Don't whistle, sing, or laugh out loud.

Don't slam pots and pans around the kitchen.

Don't wake us up to see something really great on TV.

If you live in a dorm or apartment building, you will have enough noise to contend with without adding to it.

"Bethany is one of those perky little Type A people who jumps out of bed before the alarm goes off. She forgets to turn it off and then when it starts buzzing, she is usually in the shower. I either have to lay in bed and listen to it, or get up and shut if off."

Tilly

Share responsibilities by taking turns calling the landlord, utility companies, etc., when you have a problem.

"Call the landlord, I stopped up the toilet. Call the landlord, we've got ants. Call the landlord this, and call the landlord that! I get sick and tired of hearing it! Just because your name is on the lease, doesn't mean you should have to take care of everything."

Brieann

Even when it is obvious that you really need to borrow something, ask anyway. Don't just help yourself.

"It all started when Patsy was coughing like a fool and I offered her some of my cough syrup. I told her to help herself to anything she needed — *needed* being the key word. But now, she considers everything to be community property, including my expensive perfume, so I have to hide things I don't want her using."

Danielle

Make sure your guests do not borrow anything unless it belongs to you.

"I came home late and dog-tired from my moonlighting job as a waitress, ready to fall into bed for half a night's sleep before teaching kindergarten the next day, and found that my alarm clock was missing. Unbelievable. What could that idiot I lived with have done with it?

After racing around the apartment in the dark, I found it in the spare bedroom along with her sleeping sister. But, I forgot to reset it, and was an hour late for work!"

Kris

Don't lock the deadbolt or chain the door unless you're readily available to let your roommate in.

"A pathetic creep who lived in our building kept hanging around our door, so we started locking the deadbolt. The problem was that I worked a very erratic schedule as a nurse, sometimes coming home late at night. The wretch I lived with kept locking the deadbolt whether I was home or not, so I usually ended up waking up all the neighbors and freezing to death before she would get out of bed and let me in. Finally, I got smart and started calling her to tell her when I'd be leaving work."

Anne

Don't have keys made for the convenience of your friends, family, or lovers.

Having keys made for emergencies is a sensible idea, but whoever has custody of a key should use it only when absolutely necessary. And when special circumstances warrant such use, a courteous practice would be to knock before inserting the key into the lock.

"After living together for nearly year, Sally decided to take a week's vacation. It would be a vacation for me too, knowing I didn't have to clean up after her, I could finally have total control over the channel changer, and I could take long, hot baths, a luxury I sorely missed since allowing her to move in.

The first night that I knew she was safely at least five states away, I took my freedom seriously. I stretched the TV cable across the apartment so I could watch a movie from the tub. Just as I started to relax in a mountain of fragrant bubbles, the apartment door swung open and in walked Sally's mother and sister, snickering at the sight of me. They had stopped by to retrieve a catalog that she had borrowed.

At that moment, I would have preferred living in an empty refrigerator box in an alley to living with her. I certainly would have had more privacy!

As much as her family barged in and out of our apartment, we might as well have had a revolving door installed."

Amanda

"I hate it that Regina gave her fiancée a key to our apartment. He's always vegging out on *my* couch watching sports, even when she's not here. He should be paying rent!"

Jodi

"Tonya's little sister has a key so she can stay with us, supposedly when the weather is bad. That little manipulator just uses us so she can run around all night and her parents won't know it. Then, she shows up just about the time I'm ready to shower for work and makes me late, because *she,* the non-paying tenant, is in the bathroom."

Tammy

"If I wanted somebody's parents around all the time, I would be living at home. It has become a common practice for Shawn's parents to let themselves into our apartment anytime of the day or night."

Bill

"I spent so much time away from our apartment, I didn't realize how much control I'd lost over *my half.* Marla, and her boyfriend, were away for the weekend — actually, I think it was the first time they had been out of the apartment, except for going to work. It was customary for them to be sprawled out all over the place, so that I either had to leave or feel like an intruder in my own home. It was the first time I'd ever been able to invite my boyfriend over to my place.

I was putting the finishing touches on dinner when the door swung open and in walked a guy I had never seen before! Despite my startled reaction, he had the audacity to ask what *I* was doing there. I told him that the last time I'd checked, I lived there and who was *he*?

It turned out that he was supposed to meet Marla's sister at our apartment. She had given them permission to have a little rendezvous while she away.

Needless to say, it got ugly in the end and I moved out."

Victoria

Stay out of your roommate's personal belongings.

"There was a long hill leading up to our apartment building, so I could see that now and then my bedroom light was mysteriously on. Just as I'd pull into the parking lot, the light would go off. Obviously, Robin had been in my room and I suspected she was looking through my personal papers, so I bought a strong box with a lock. After that, you could cut the tension with a knife. She knew she was caught, and then made up a flimsy excuse about wanting to move so she could live closer to work. I didn't care. Once the trust is gone, things are never the same."

Jenna

"I just about jumped out of my skin when Sandy asked if I'd found my birthstone ring. I hadn't told *anyone* I'd lost it, but I remembered I had written about it in my personal journal that I kept under my bed. The temptation to get revenge consumed me.

I began to fabricate stories in my daily accounts, knowing she was reading them. One by one, I stacked up clues alluding to a secret affair with her boyfriend. As she became angry and frustrated, I couldn't help but feel completely smug about it. She lost her boyfriend and my friendship as a result."

Jodi

"Nothing is ever missing, but it gives me the heebie-jeebies knowing Paula paws through my things when I'm not home. I feel as if I have no privacy at all."

Jackie

Don't you dare run out and get a pet without discussing it first.

"Sheena bought a gerbil, which seemed like no big deal until it started squeezing its way out of the cage. That little varmint left droppings everywhere, and then chewed a hole in a brand new outfit I had laying in a paper bag on my closet floor.

Then she wanted to get a cat. I can still hear her asking me, *What trouble can a cat be?* I agreed, thinking it might catch that darn gerbil anyway. Now let me tell you just what trouble a cat *can* be.

No matter whose cat it is, everyone's furniture and clothing will be covered with cat hair. Everything you own, from the waist down, will be shredded. You might become immune to the smell of a litter box, but your guests won't. And, you won't be able to cook or eat without that furry beast jumping up on your table or countertops, or incessantly yowling throughout the entire meal."

Sami

"The lease clearly stated that we could not have any pets, but Kay bought a dog anyway, saying it was a *show dog*, as if that made a difference. Even though we shampooed the carpets after we moved out, the landlord kept our security deposit. I think that's why he never told us to get rid of it, so he could keep our deposit.

By rights, she should have reimbursed me for my half, but she refused because apparently, I hadn't made my feelings clear when the stupid mutt moved in."

Angie

Even if your roommate swears you won't have to do a thing, don't agree to get a pet unless you're willing to help take care of it.

"It's not that I don't like animals, it's just that my philosophy is that if you don't have a pet, you don't have to take care of it. Of course Janice swore, like a ten-year-old, that she would do everything herself.

It wasn't even a week after she got a dog that he woke me up whining and slobbering all over my face because he needed to go out. Janice was out on a date, and hadn't been home in over 12 hours. Of course now I'm in love with that furry beast, but he's a horrible inconvenience to me."

Sandy

Don't pretend to be enthusiastic about getting a pet, and then treat it inhumanely because you didn't want it in the first place.

"Jeff hated my dog, so he would pour beer into his water dish to be mean. I took him to the vet, thinking he was sick because he was acting funny and peeing on the carpet. When I found out he was just drunk, I had my parents keep him until I could find another place to live."

Beau

"Corey worked as a bartender until two or three in the morning, so he slept while I was at work during the day. For the longest time, I couldn't figure out why my birds kept dying. One day I came home sick from work and found the cage on the porch in the freezing cold. He said he couldn't sleep with their chirping and squawking."

Bob

"The neighbors are ready to tar and feather me. Bill was afraid of my snake, so he took the cage outside and left the door open. He tried to say it got loose in the house, but there's a lady next door who always has her nose smashed against a window night and day, and she witnessed the whole thing. It's cold outside, so I'm sure he's slithered into someone's basement by now."

Sam

Don't leave your laundry rotting in the washer or dryer. Get it out when the cycle is finished.

"We purposely looked for a place to rent that had a washer and dryer so we wouldn't have to go to the laundry mat, but Aaron drives me crazy by not finishing his own loads. After a couple of months of folding his clothes, I got smart and started piling his stuff on top of the machines. I'm not his mother."

Ken

"During the spring and summer, I umpire somewhere almost every night to make extra money. Paul knows that, and he knows I need to wash my uniform as soon as I get home so I can dry it in the morning before work. It never fails, I get home and he has left a load sitting in the bottom of the washer. It's the simple inconsiderate things that get to you."

Robert

Ruin your laundry if you want, but don't ruin someone else's.

"Ed played softball all day in his favorite jeans and then tried to tumble the dirt out in the dryer so he could wear them that night. I didn't know it and dried a load of whites. How stupid can you be?"

Bob

"Tammy dyed a pair of jeans black and left the muck all over the inside of the washer. Luckily I discovered it before I threw anything in, but it took hours to clean up the mess."

Carrie

Don't let your irresponsible behavior become a burden to others.

"Normally before leaving for work, I would turn the coffee maker off. After noticing that Jenny was drinking whatever was left over, I thought it would be a nice gesture to leave the pot on so the coffee would still be hot when she got up. As you can probably guess, she left the pot on, and I came home to a smoldering mess. The leftover coffee was burning and the smoke alarm was screeching. Of course I told her about it, but she shrugged it off, so from then on I turned if off when I left. She began turning it back on and soon she did the same thing again.

That was it for me, so I started dumping out whatever was left and running hot soapy water into the pot. In retaliation, she dumped the soapy water down in the coffee maker! How immature can you be?"

Mindy

"I had to stop renting videos because Tammy would take them over to her boyfriends and forget to bring them back. Then I had to pay a huge fine for returning them late."

Cathy

"One of our neighbors called me at work to tell me our yard looked like it was flooding, so there might a break in our water line. Dan had washed his truck and then left the hose running. He can be so ignorant at times."

Barry

If you snore, shut your door.

"Jeremy didn't want his bedroom door shut at night, but he sounded like an idling German tank. I had to tape record the noise before he'd believe how offensive it was."

Steve

Remember that whatever you do to annoy the neighbors will be a reflection on the people you live with.

Like it or not, all of you will be viewed by your neighbors as one entity. In other words, you are a package deal even though only one of you may be causing problems.

"The landlord keeps calling and saying, *You girls are playing your stereo too loud, you girls this, and you girls that.* It's not me, it's Teri! She is the one who always gets us into trouble, and she doesn't care."

Laura

"One night after a bachelor party, Bob came home and threw up in the hallway of our apartment building, right in front of our door. Suddenly, people on our floor, who had been quite chatty before, began to cold shoulder me. I'm sure it was because they had to walk by that putrid mess every day, and he wouldn't clean it up.

He walked around it as if it weren't there, and when we moved out, I had to chisel the remnants up with a screwdriver and scrub brush. It left a stain and we lost our security deposit just because of that."

Ted

Don't touch other people's makeup.

"As a nurse, I'm a fanatic about germs. I double-glove at work and always keep a mask dangling from my neck in case I need it. You can't imagine my disgust when I discovered Brenda had been using my lipstick!"

Debbie

Before you agree to a shared food arrangement, figure the odds of it working out.

When busy people agree to take turns grocery shopping, menu planning, and cooking, they often find it is an agreement they can't, or are unwilling, to live up to. But take heart. You don't really have to be all that clever to bow out.

"All I had to do was pretend I was going on a diet. Stan was eating ninety-nine percent of the food we bought and I couldn't stand his cooking, so I was losing weight anyway."

Gordon

"About once a week, I would have liked to have slipped off to the mall after work, but I couldn't do it if it was my turn to cook. I started volunteering for random hours at work until it became too much of a hassle to coordinate meals."

Tracey

"One of the privileges of being young, single, and self-supportive should be being able to eat whatever you want, whenever you want. After I passed up a great deal on a cashmere sweater because I had to spend the money on groceries, that was it for me. I didn't want to eat expensive cuts of red meat. I wanted to eat peanut butter!

I decided I didn't care if I hurt Cheri's feelings or not, I had to be brutally honest, or remain miserable. It turned out that she was unhappy too, so we divided up the shelves in the fridge and have lived happily ever after."

Martina

Don't sabotage your roommate's diet.

"Janelle is blatantly transparent in her efforts to ruin my diet. I can't stay home on a weekend night and relax without her bugging me to order a pizza when I've already eaten something healthy and light. She leaves bags of candy and bowls of chips out *for company*, which she used to hide from me until she became envious that I was losing weight.

I'm also sick of hearing about how popular the oversized woman is becoming when it is clearly a cover for her inability to control her eating."

Cindy

Unless you are Richard Simmons, don't try to dictate what your roommate eats.

"Leanne certainly has a firm grasp of the obvious. If she says one more time, *You know if you wouldn't eat so much junk, you would lose weight,* I'm going to scream. When someone says something like that, do you think, *Wow, what a revelation! I must be fat because I eat too much!* No, what you really think is, *You're saying that I have no self-control,* or, *You disapprove of me because I'm fat.*"

Tina

"Charles was so obsessed with healthy eating that he hung a chart of the basic food groups on the refrigerator and kept a journal of every fat gram he ingested. Frankly, I was impressed. He was quite a physical specimen and had a ton of energy and willpower. I made the mistake of thinking I could adhere to his program and suddenly, I took on the personality of a three-year-old, trying to sneak cookies into the house. He monitored everything I ate, even *after* I admitted I was throwing in the towel. It took awhile to figure out that the temptation of the food I kept around was killing him.

I couldn't believe myself when one night, as he walked in, I crushed a bag of potato chips under the couch to hide them. That was it. I pulled it back out and we both burst out laughing when I asked him if he wanted to sniff the bag. He left me alone after that."

Dan

Don't start out thinking you'll get used to something that will clearly be a problem for you. Speak up and get it out in the open.

"I walked into our apartment just in time to stop Karen from taking her first snip out of her boyfriend's hair in the middle of our kitchen floor. Without a lot of fluff, I explained that under no circumstances could I tolerate her cutting hair in our apartment. My ex-husband had been a barber, and for years I had lived with little pieces of hair working their way into everything — my food, my clothes, and even between my sheets.

I felt like a shrew while telling her all this, but surprisingly, she just laughed and took her boyfriend and her scissors outside. It's a shame that people can't express their needs more often, because most people really will understand and comply without feeling put out."

Marilee

Be adamant about what you want, but don't be ridiculous.

"When Al told me that *lights out* would be at ten o'clock on weekdays, I thought, *What is this, church camp?* He claimed he couldn't sleep with any noise whatsoever, so I'd have to go to bed when he did. That was a pretty good indication of things to come, because he turned out to be a real screwball in general."

Daniel

"The first girl I shared an apartment with never washed her own dishes, so I was elated when Sara insisted I wash my dishes immediately after eating.

But it turned out that her idea of washing dishes included mopping the floor and drying out the sink. She definitely had a cleaning sickness."

Brandi

"Janet demanded a 24-hour notification if I would be having anyone over. Apparently, she wasn't very spontaneous, but I complied until she started having friends drop by unannounced.

She did the same thing with the bathroom, wanting me to clean out the tub every time I showered, yet she never did it."

Kelly

Take responsibility for your mistakes. If you break it, replace it, pay for it, or clean it up.

"My drinking glasses all disappeared one by one, but Candy never fessed up to breaking them or ever offered to replace them. I knew she was guilty because I could hear the glass rattling around in the bottom of the trash can."

Della

"Christy has this obsession with wanting the windows left open all day long from spring through fall. First of all, this is just an open invitation for uninvited guests. Luckily, any thieves in our neighborhood must hold other daytime positions, because we've yet to be hit, but I worry about it constantly.

The other problem is with the weather. Twice, I've returned home to rain soaked carpet and a wet couch. I haven't felt the need to relay my disapproval verbally. *I* certainly would have gotten the message the first time I came home to find my roommate sopping up water with bath towels and running fans everywhere. But no, not her!

The icing on the cake was last week when we were both at a baseball game it began to rain. She said, *Oh gee, I left the windows open.* Then she raised her umbrella, and just sat there. I left the game, shut the windows, and started packing."

Toni

How to Keep from Being Screwed by a Scrooge

(If I Were Rich, Do You Think I'd Be Living with You?)

When it comes to finances, don't foolishly believe that splitting the bills will be a cut-and-dried issue. Your spending habits will never be parallel, especially when it comes to flipping off light switches and deciding what to blow your nose on.

Major financial dissention is one of the top dogs in killing otherwise solid relationships, (especially marriages), yet so are the small, undisclosed suspicions relating to money which may seem too petty to mention. You may have been taught to "tear off a square" when using the bathroom, while you envision your roommate mummifying him- or herself every time you hear the toilet flush.

The bottom line is that there are no insignificant issues when it comes to money. Let's better the odds that you won't be taken for a ride by establishing some rules.

When initially renting a place to live, divide up the responsibilities of signing utility contracts, and have everyone sign the lease, if possible.

If everything is registered under your name, and your name only, everyone can abandon ship whenever they please, leaving you financially responsible. Conversely, if everything is in your name, you can get rid co-tenants without too many hassles. You won't have to have utilities changed over to your name, or worry about someone turning the electricity off without warning you.

"Sally moved out in a snit and didn't pay her share of final bills, but it didn't matter. I was smart when we moved in and had her pay half of all the deposits so I could keep all of the refunds in case this happened."

April

Place a tab of what everyone owes in the same place every month and write a due date on it.

Then you don't have to discuss it. Nobody likes talking about finances, so put a list of how much is owed in the same spot every month.

"I put everything in an envelope and leave it on her dresser. She writes one check, puts it back in the envelope and lays it on my dresser. We never discuss money, ever. It's nice."

Maddie

"I lay a list by the phone and everyone signs their name after they have given me their check. There are eight of us, so I have to keep an accurate tab of everything. No one can use the phone without noticing who has paid and who hasn't."

Kelly

"You should always ask to see the monthly bills. One night, when Joe and I were out with friends, someone asked me if I noticed that every time it was his turn to buy a round, he either went to the bathroom or made some excuse why he had to leave. That was when I first suspicioned he might be cheating me on bills. The next time he asked for a check, I asked to see the utility bills, and you should have seen him squirm. He said he threw them all away as soon as he mailed the checks and was just waiting for my money to reimburse himself. I contacted the utility companies, told them my story, and was able to get enough information to estimate that he owned me at least a free month's rent. Then I moved out."

Doug

Designate a specific day of the month when all money should be paid to whomever pays the bills.

The person responsible for writing checks has the right to expect everyone to pay up several days before the bills are due. That way, the money can be deposited in time to insure that the checks will clear the bank.

"Sue puts off paying me until one month turns into the next, and then she argues about the amount I have meticulously kept track of and recorded. If she would just pay me once a month on a regular basis, we wouldn't have this problem!"

D.C.

"You want to watch people who always pay you months in arrears. I lived in a house with six other girls, and two of them moved home and stiffed the rest of us for over $500."

Carmen

"Here I am, 22 years old, and living from check to check on my first job, but having a wonderful time out on my own. The only problem is, I have to skimp sometimes to be sure to meet bills because of Pete. He recklessly spends his paycheck and then runs out of money just about the time everything is due. I'm having the phone disconnected and keeping my cell phone. Maybe he'll get the message — no pun intended."

Billy

Divide the rent and utilities equally unless you have specifically worked out another agreement.

"When we moved in, we flipped for the master bedroom which includes a walk-in closet and a private bathroom with a garden tub. I pay seventy-five bucks extra a month voluntarily. I can afford it, and believe me, it is worth it. This way, I feel totally guilt-free."

Ned

"My share of the water bill increased substantially after months of being the same amount. I called the water company and found out that either my roommate was cheating me, or he was lacking in mathematical skills. That sneak was making me pay more than my fair share. I called all the utility companies to verify everything else and found out he was doing it all along. You should ask to see the bill before paying your share."

Joe

"After I moved in, I got the shock of my life when Patricia said she thought I should pay two-thirds of the rent because I put my things in the extra closet without asking her! I told her I'd stack my crap in a corner first."

Laura

Don't expect your roommate to contribute more financially due to having a better paying job, family support, or a sudden windfall.

"When my father died, the first thing Jenny said was, *Bet you'll get rid of that old piece of junk you're driving because of your inheritance.* She couldn't have been more wrong. The only thing I was about to get rid of was her because I had listened to her jealous comments about my hard-working family for two years. And, I was sick and tired of having to pick up the tab when she claimed to be broke."

Justine

"Nathan thought he was my favorite charity. Just because I made more money than he did, he expected me to buy all the toilet paper and food. He whined about not having any money until I couldn't stand it anymore and moved out."

Travis

"I feel like I'm always getting screwed financially. Tom started getting a chip on his shoulder when I got promoted at work. The kookiest idea he ever came up with deciding to pay me a quarter every time he used the phone instead of splitting the bill. He says he hardly ever makes any calls, but it's the funniest thing — every time I try to call him, the line is busy."

Ryan

"Why do lazy slugs think they have the right to complain about someone making more money? If someone has a better job than you do, it is probably for a reason. Maybe that person has more education or has developed better people skills or a good work ethic. Or maybe that person was in the right place at the right time, has more experience, knows the right people, or doesn't mind smooching a few rear ends. Whatever!

The point is, successful people do not want to listen to someone griping about the size of their paycheck. I refuse to spend another winter wrapped up in an electric blanket because Tiffany keeps turning down the heat, saying that I should kick in more for the gas bill if I want it warmer in our apartment. As if she would rather freeze than pay a few extra dollars a month!"

Veronica

Log all your long distance calls to prevent discrepancies and to save time figuring your portion of the phone bill.

"The dimwit I lived with would call Botswana to see if they were having a sale on Tiki lamps, then forget about it and deny making the call when the bill came. Of course the phone was in my name, so I was the lucky one who got stuck paying for all of the calls that she couldn't remember making. I started buying phone cards, which was a pain, but then I knew that *every* long distance call was hers."

Melanie

"With five roommates, I was forever tying to get everyone to own up to their long distance calls. I got so mad, I unplugged the phone and hid it in my room. Of course someone bought another phone and just plugged it in the jack. Then I had the phone service disconnected, bought a cell phone, and told them they could get their own blankety-blank phone service."

Mike

Always make a record of, and pay for, any long distance calls *your* guests make.

"Courtney's fiancée starting using our phone to make long distance calls soon after their engagement. I had no qualms about him doing that, as long as she took care of collecting the money or paid for the calls herself. When the first bill came, I circled his calls, and she told me to ask *him* for the money. I said I most certainly would not, so she reluctantly asked him, making a big hairy deal out of it in front of me. She said, *Heidi is afraid to ask you for the money for those long distance calls you made.* Then they had this huge fight because he thought he shouldn't have to pay for them since he paid for all of their dates.

This happened six months before they got married, and by the time the wedding rolled around, she still hadn't paid me. She even had the gall to say once, *Gee, I can't believe Joe hasn't paid you for those calls yet.*

For a wedding gift, I photocopied the phone bills and wrote *PAID!!!* in huge black letters."

Heidi

"The ding bat I lived with let our neighbors use our telephone, and unbeknownst to her, they were making long distance calls. The phone was in my name, but I made her pay up since she was the one who gave them permission."

Marlene

If your computer is off limits, then *you* should pay for an extra phone line.

"We are permitted personal use of our computers at work during breaks, lunch, and after hours, so I haven't felt the need to buy a PC to use at home. Sherri has one, but I'm not allowed to touch it, and she feels no qualms about tying up the phone line all night. If she'd allow me a little computer time, I wouldn't care. I think she should pay for an extra line."

Paula

Insist on paying for your costly mistakes.

"Robin lost her key chain, bearing our address, in a popular bar. I was scared to death, so I had the locks changed. A month later, she recovered her keys, so she argued that she shouldn't have to reimburse me for half the locksmith's bill. How would she like it if I had the original locks reinstalled? Someone could have made a copy of those keys."

Helen

"No one had ever told Fred to clean the lint trap in the dryer, so inevitably, it caught on fire. He didn't care; it was *my* dryer. So he never skipped a beat. He just started going to the laundry mat and never offered to help buy a new one."

Ted

Don't expect automatic support of your financial ventures.

"Have you ever known someone who is always selling something so you try to avoid them all the time? Unfortunately, I lived with someone like that. First, she peddled expensive cosmetics, then kitchenware, and then tacky trash to decorate with. At first, I bought a few things to make her happy, then I found a way to get her to quit pressuring me. I asked her to get a few things wholesale for me *since we were such great friends.*"

Heather

"When Sara began selling health food and vitamins, she turned into a real huckster. She had the nerve to go through my address book, without my permission, and called everyone telling them I had suggested they might be interested in her products. I was furious!"

Kim

Don't use your roommate for your financial advantage.

"One of the perks of my job at a department store is a 25% employee discount. Beth browses on a continuous basis and then has me buy things for her, which is a big no-no. I'm paranoid that I'll get caught, but she tells me I'm being silly. If my manager finds out, I'll get fired."

Frannie

"About two months after Bill moved out, I received an insurance bill from the company where he used to work. I never purchased insurance in my entire life from them, so I called to see what the deal was.

It seemed that Bill was able to net the commission before the premium came due, so he had forged my name on a policy."

Ted

Don't borrow money.

"Bob frequently borrowed money *until he could get to the ATM*. It would only be a few dollars here and there, but he would wait for what seemed like forever, to pay me back. In the meantime, I'd get mad thinking he had forgotten."

Kevin

"How could I say no? If I refused, I felt like a heel going out to dinner or buying anything frivolous while she was digging under the couch cushions for enough change to ride the bus to work. It wasn't my fault she couldn't manage her money."

Lora

"I couldn't believe the day Martina bragged about buying a two-hundred dollar handbag at Bloomingdale's for 50 percent off. At the time, she still owed me three hundred dollars, which she had borrowed two months earlier while between jobs. I was steamed to say the least."

Kara

Need to borrow a car? Don't even ask. (Don't steal it either.)

"You know the drill. Tom's car was continuously in the shop, so he used mine. Sure, he filled it up with gas, but then he got into a hit-and-run accident and my insurance went through the roof. Do you think he'll pay for that?"

Ben

Never be late in kicking in for your share of the bills no matter what. If you don't have the money, then you need to find a cheaper place to live.

"Every month, Charlie became later and later paying his share of the bills until he was technically an entire month behind. It was funny that he always seemed to have enough cash to buy beer and go to the dog track every weekend."

Gus

Offer restitution for things you use that you didn't pay for.

"I have allergies, so I buy boxes and boxes of Kleenex, which my room-mates help themselves to and never replace. It might sound petty, but now I hide them so I know I'll always have some left."

Robin

"When Tonya and I first moved in together, I asked if she would like to go halfsies to have the local paper delivered. She thought not. She could read the paper at work for free. I said *fine*, but I would be getting it anyway.

First, I noticed she had been digging it out of the trash. Then, as she would put it, she began *glancing through it* when I was finished with it. One thing led to another until she was grabbing the paper off of the doormat and reading it before I could get to it, or it would disappear altogether! This was more than annoying, but I decided not to make a big deal out of it because she started paying the paperboy once in awhile…*or so I thought*!

One evening, the paperboy pounded on our door and told me he was dropping me as a customer because I was six weeks behind in payment. Whenever I thought of it, I would leave an envelope with money out for him, and the rest of the time, I assumed Tonya was paying him. I told him exactly that, and he informed me that she had told him on more than one occasion to come back later and collect from me.

I came unglued. I had the paper stopped and started picking it up on the way home from work. And as a further barb, I would staple it shut when I finished reading it, or I would throw it in the trash and dump wet, soggy garbage all over it."

Missy

If you borrow something, replace it before it will be missed.

"Just this morning I cut my ankle shaving. I grabbed my box of Band-Aids and it was empty. Exasperated, I reached for a cotton ball to at least stop the bleeding, and the bag was empty. Then, I decided to just wrap it with toilet paper, but I'm sure you've guessed by now, that the roll was empty too.

Incapable of making any rational decisions, I proceeded to take one of my fussy roommate's pink towels and used it to stop the bleeding. I dare her to say a word!"

Greta

"Sally had been using my computer and used up the ink cartridge in the printer and didn't replace it. I had less than an hour to get ready for a job interview, and couldn't print out an extra copy of my resume. I bombed the interview, and I'm sure it was just because I was still fuming from her inconsiderate behavior."

Karen

If you don't have an arrangement for sharing food, then don't help yourself to anything you didn't buy.

Keep your food on separate shelves in the cupboards and refrigerator to avoid confusion. If you use something you didn't purchase, replace it immediately.

"Joe acted as if he was in a restaurant where he could use all the condiments for free. I told him to buy his own or take turns buying them when we ran out."

Jason

"Chad would drink all my milk and set the empty carton back in the fridge. I started taping the spout closed so he would get the hint."

Bobby

"Do you realize how expensive spices are? It drives me crazy trying to remember to check and see if I have something like chili powder before I shop for the rest of the ingredients."

Peggy

Don't complain about the overuse of utilities unless the monthly bills show a substantial increase.

"Don't argue about utilities because you will become meter maids, trying to prove that the other person uses more of one thing than you do of the other. Deanna claimed my showers were too long. I countered with her abuse of electricity by leaving the TV, stereo, lights, curling iron, and anything else with an on/off switch running 24 hours a day. One weekend I looked all over the building for her to see if I could turn the fans off in her room because I was getting cold, and she had gone home for the weekend! She said she left them running because her bedroom stunk."

Penny

"I take two showers a day, one for work, and the other after I work out. The scumbag I live with seems to have one goal in life, and that is to try and stop me from doing this. He complains that I'm running the water bill up, but every month, our water bill is exactly the same: *the minimum charge*."

Tom

"We live in a basement apartment so it is always cool in the summer, but Meredith cranks up the air conditioning until you can't walk barefooted on the linoleum floor in the kitchen. I complain because our electric bills are astronomical, but she still does it. I'm not going to last very long with her."

Mary

"Beth runs water continuously in the kitchen sink while she washes the dishes and wipes off the counter tops. This can go on for an hour. Then she has the nerve to flip my bedroom light off, even when I go into the bathroom for a minute or two. She's driving me insane!"

June

"No one can top the penny-pincher I live with. He suggested in a round about way that I should use *the can* at work as much as I can because you save on water and toilet paper. And when it's his turn to buy toilet paper, guess where he steals it from."

Brian

Buy your share of disposable items.

You should take turns purchasing, or split the cost of:

toilet paper
paper towels
napkins
trash bags
light bulbs
message pads and pens
dish washing liquid
cleaning products (and use them!)
envelopes and stamps for mailing bills

You will be better off if you do not share:

laundry detergent
dryer sheets
bleach
spray starch
bar soap
shampoo and cream rinse
hair spray
toothpaste
mouth wash
over the counter medicine
tampons and sanitary napkins
food and drinks, including condiments

Beware when someone launches a big idea that will include you. There might be hidden costs.

"When Leah came up with the bright idea of having a New Year's Eve party in our apartment, I jumped on the band wagon. I liked the thought of being able to party and then not having to drive anywhere, and our friends could stay until they sobered up.

But the next thing I knew, she had ordered a hundred helium balloons and enough food, from a pricey deli, to feed 75 people. She bought beer, liquor, and expensive mixers, intending to provide everything. I thought we'd have a potluck and go BYOB.

I nearly stroked out when she presented me with half the bill. She rationalized that it would enhance my social life, but it didn't work out that way. Only twenty-some people showed up, got smashed, and left, and never reciprocated with an invitation for *me* anywhere.

I had to forfeit my annual spring vacation with my childhood friend at an ocean front hotel to catch up financially."

Gerry

"Rosie's father spoiled her by taking her out to extravagant restaurants once or twice a month to try and win back her affection after abandoning her family when she was a child. When he would come by to pick her up, she would always try to cajole me into going with them because she couldn't stand him.

Feeling lonely on my birthday, I gave in. I guess I was presumptuous to have expected her father to pick up the tab for me too. I was thunderstruck when he told me what my share of the check was. Luckily, I had my credit card with me, but it was embarrassing to ask the waiter to separate my bill from theirs."

Angelic

"Cathy was really into decorating our apartment, but I couldn't stand the tacky looking junk she bought. Instead of adding to her indiscriminate clutter, I started saving my money for other things.

Then the shower curtain tore, and she hinted that I should buy one. I told her to go ahead and get one and I'd pay half. She came home with a very expensive bath ensemble that I wouldn't have used in an outhouse, that I had to help pay for."

Terri

Don't break the landlord's rules, especially if your name is not on the lease.

"I'll never forget returning home from work and finding my landlord sitting on the steps waiting for me. My softhearted roommate had found a stray puppy whining in the parking lot, and brought it inside to care for it until she could find the owner.

The darn thing had fleas, so we had to "bug bomb" the whole place. We lived in an old duplex, so the neighbors had evidently gotten a whiff of the fumes and called him, implicating me because the lease was in my name.

He didn't throw us out, but even though I left the place immaculate when we moved, I lost my entire security deposit."

Samantha

Don't declare war on your landlord over petty issues, dragging your cohabitants down with you.

In the end, your landlord will win by retaining your security deposit, evicting you, or taking you to small claims court.

"The first time Kathy let a dish cloth slip into the garbage disposal jamming it, I called the landlord and he cheerfully fixed it. The second time, I was too embarrassed to call him, so I paid a plumber to untangle it. Even though she was the moron who did it, she wouldn't split the bill with me and subtracted the amount from the rent check with a written explanation. When the landlord said it would come off of our security deposit, she threatened to withhold our last months rent check.

What an ignoramus. We lost our entire security deposit which was more than a month's rent."

Ellen

"Bob thought we should leave our apartment a wreck when me moved out to *punish* our landlord for charging such high rent. Good grief, we knew how much the rent was when we moved in. He just didn't want to have to do anything other than pack his bags and split. I cleaned everything up anyway so we would get our deposit back. The bad part was that the lease was in his name and he got the check and only gave me half."

Rick

Stay on good terms with your landlord.

"Previous tenants had ticked off a man living in a house next to our apartment building by driving through his back yard, rather than taking the time to maneuver their cars out of the parking lot. In retaliation, he built a storage shed blocking the view from our front window. Our landlord told us that was why our rent was so cheap, and asked us to please not do anything to antagonize him any further.

Sally paid no heed to warning. In fact, one of her favorite pastimes became flicking cigarette butts in the old man's woodpile hoping it would catch on fire.

At Christmas time, she snuck into his yard and whacked off pine branches to decorate our apartment. Of course when the landlord came pounding at the door, she was no where around. What was I supposed to say when he asked me if we had been cutting down those branches? I was standing there plucking pine needles out of my socks while he was talking."

Julie

Don't jeopardize your roommate's chances of getting his or her share of the security deposit back by mistreating your apartment.

"I was furious when I didn't get my half of our deposit back. I know it was because of Carrie. She and her boyfriend would have sexual rendezvous that ended up destroying everything. In the bathroom alone, they ripped down a towel bar and the shower curtain rod, jerked the countertop around the sink loose from the wall, and ruined the carpeting by sloshing water everywhere."

Kim

"The galloping gourmet I lived with ruined our stove because he boiled food too fast and the liquid ran over the sides of the pots into the stove, damaging the heating mechanisms. He also broiled meat until there was no hope of ever getting the oven clean again. So *we* lost *our* deposit."

Andie

"Sue used our countertops as a cutting board. By the time we moved out, she had chopped them to smithereens."

Beth

"It is a monthly ritual for Tina to break something we can't fix ourselves. This month she broke her key off in the lock on the door. I've lost all hope of ever getting our deposit back."

Dan

"I got my deposit back, but only after I shampooed the carpets with no help from my lousy sister. She and her boyfriend used the living room carpet as a table cloth."

Sherry

In a romantic relationship, bills do not have to be split down the middle.

Income is usually lopsided in a marriage anyway, so if you limit yourself to economically equal partners, you'll cheat yourself out of a larger pool of potential mates.

"Randall was so generous, I knew I'd eventually marry him. I was looking for a mate that would support me someday if I decided to have children and be a stay-at-home mom."

Liz

"I'm no fool. I make up for not paying what I really should on monthly bills by taking care of Kevin. That way, he really doesn't care how much I shop for myself!"

Saundra

Unless you truly enjoy annoying people, don't be a pesky scrooge about money.

"The tax on our long distance calls drives Andy crazy. Rather than just splitting the amount, he will work for hours calculating the amount charged per call. I've offered to pay the whole darn thing if he'd just stop fretting about it."

Shawn

"Paula is the epitome of stinginess. She can't even mail a payment without charging me half the cost of the stamp."

Natalie

"I was mortified when Darlene tried to force me to deduct the price of a lousy light bulb I replaced outside our door from our monthly rent check.

I know I could have called the landlord to replace it, but it was simpler to do it myself."

Trinda

Air your feelings about frugality, but not without a fair proposal.

Even though you may be equal when it comes to earning power, a tight-fisted cohort may prove to be as big a headache as one who cannot meet monthly bills.

"Doug was such a tight wad, it didn't make any difference that he made twice the money I did. He drove a clunker that was in the shop more than it was out, and I reluctantly had become his personal taxi service. He also tried to control the thermostat so I froze to death in the winter and had sweat running down my back all summer.

Body language wasn't cutting it, so I started getting on him good-naturedly until he finally came around and agreed to a more tolerable setting. I've adjusted by wearing more clothes in the winter and less in the summer."

Adam

"Evie was a psycho about the way she spent her money. She insisted on buying fancy napkins that were in with the current season and other ridiculous things we didn't need. Sick of it, when it was my turn to grocery shop, I bought a large economy roll of paper towels. It made her mad so she used them to clean. I could have bought a car with the money she wasted, and I told her so.

That's when we decided to further divide what we would be responsible to purchase. I'd use my cheap papers towels, and she could wipe her twenty-dollar lipstick off with her ten-dollar napkins."

Bethany

Social Protocol

(What you never knew you needed to know.)

Not all perpetrators of social transgressions are purposely vicious or blindly self-indulgent. Some are just flat-out simpletons who somehow missed learning the rudimentary rules of etiquette while growing up. And if you are dead set on proving to the rest of the world that your cohabitant is indeed a certified idiot, what will this mission accomplish?

Earlier it was mentioned that one of the benefits of having a roommate is the prospect of enriching your social life. Even if your outside lives never mesh, you should aim to enjoy one another's company, adding another pleasant dimension to your personal life. So pity the poor soul who was raised under a rock and vow to help him or her gain the sense of perspective that others have given you. Stop expecting all your assumptions to be assumed and stop responding to appalling behavior with an abrasive attitude.

People are reactionary by nature. The treatment you get will be the basis for the treatment you give. If you are consciously aware of this fact, you can break a bad spell by reacting calmly and with kindness. This doesn't mean you're supposed to roll over and play dead. If you do, you're sending the message that his or her behavior is acceptable to you. It's just that a screaming match doesn't solve anything, it will only create yet another issue: How you *speak* to one another.

Before you bookmark this section, leave it on the coffee table and run, maybe you'd better take a gander first. Sometimes we fail to detect our own personality flaws until we discover them in others.

Don't ask to be fixed up with a friend or relative.

"Marsha really put me on the spot when she revealed she was in love with my brother. I knew she didn't stand a chance with him; he frequently made fun of her for being such an airhead and she outweighed him by at least fifty pounds. But what if he *was* interested? They would probably date a while, break up, and then it would strain my relationship with both of them.

Anyway, my brother has stopped coming over because she throws herself at him and he can't take the pressure. I can't take it either, so I'm thinking about moving out."

Pam

Save your idiotic flirting for your own romantic interests.

"It is less than amusing to me that Patricia is either parading around half nude in front of my boyfriend, or she is modeling something silky she bought on sale and *just has to show us*. This is a person who lived in a pair of sweat pants and a stained T-shirt until I started dating Bill."

Candi

"Nothing makes a woman more territorial than another woman throwing herself at her man. My girlfriend's roommate does it all the time by trying to engage me in private conversations with her."

Mike

"One evening Dean kept whispering in my girlfriends' ear, and then he would look at me and laugh. I could tell she was annoyed, so I said, *Hello,*

I'm in the ro-o-o-o-om! Then I spotted a magazine in the bathroom, open to an article about how to pick up women. I figure he probably read about this stupid tactic and was now practicing on her. What a lunatic."

Joey

"I don't get much time alone with Susan, and the egomaniac I live with monopolizes her every time she comes over. She thinks he is obnoxious, but she doesn't have a mean bone in her body and is afraid he's just lonely. Before she finishes answering one question, he has asked the next. I can't help but think he's trying to *woo* her away from me."

Tim

When it is obvious that someone is visibly engrossed in something, either shut up or leave the room.

"I can't even read the newspaper, let alone a good book, without Teri yapping and interrupting me. I have to hide in my bedroom to get any peace and quiet."

Tonda

"If I ever finish the sweater I'm knitting, I'm sure one sleeve will be longer than the other because I keep losing count of the stitches. How do you politely tell someone to shut their trap?"

Lola

Keep your nose out of mail that isn't addressed to you.

"My ornery sister knew that Terri was one of the nosiest people on earth, so she would tease her by sending *me* fake love letters, tucking in the flaps instead of sealing the envelopes. How obvious can you be?

Then she fudged a letter from a mail-order bride company informing me that my perfect match had been found. She even included a picture of a real stud standing on a snowy mountainside in his snowshoes and underpants. This cured her of her annoying, snoopy habit once she figured out my sister was making a fool out of her."

Mary Anne

"I shop a great deal by mail, and frequently receive catalogs and discount certificates. Susan confiscates them, even though they are addressed to me, and sometimes even fills out the order blanks. One time I was at her sister's apartment and found one laying on her coffee table that I hadn't even seen yet!"

Toby

"I caught Tom reading a letter from my father. Now *that's* crossing the line of decency."

Adam

"If I ever need to know the balance on my credit card account, I can just ask Jerri. She doesn't even bother to put my mail back in the envelopes."

Alicia

Write down phone messages and place them beside the phone.

"This includes calls when the caller says, *Never mind, I'll call back later.* I could have guessed that a guy I had been dying to go out with was trying to call me, and I would have waited around if Janet would have just told me someone was trying to get a hold of me. I ran into him a month later and he told me I was never home, and now he's dating someone else."

Maddie

If you are lazy, tired, or mad about something and refuse to take phone messages, then don't answer the phone. Screwing around with someone's personal life is the ultimate injustice.

"Jamie would casually mention to me that someone had called, just about the time you're thinking it is too late to call anyone back. Sometimes she would remember the name, and other times not, and would slowly recall bits and pieces, driving me to the brink of insanity.

I started writing down every stinking detail of her calls, sometimes verbatim, trying to make a point, even though her sister and boyfriend called several times a day. She finally told me that her nose was out of joint because earlier I hadn't bothered to tell her every single time they'd called. That's why she had stopped taking my messages. So, I was the one who was wrong to begin with.

We've decided to get Caller ID. Then I won't have to pick up the phone for all her trivial calls."

Sara

Show respect for other's religious beliefs, traditions, and customs.

It is normal to be curious about someone's heritage, but you are walking on thin ice if you dispute or question the validity of someone's life-long affiliation.

"I get sick and tired of being lectured about how ignorant the Catholic religion is because they allow gambling and drinking. I grew up Catholic, I will always be a Catholic, and as long as the Pope says it's all right, I will keep on drinking beer and playing bingo. So there."

Jackie

"I'm a Jew from Brooklyn, and I live with a girl I met in college that was raised at the opposite end of the spectrum — by strict, Southern

Baptists. Her naivete is wildly entertaining. When my ex-boyfriend and I had a huge fight and he had told me to *go to the showers,* she started crying when she found out what that meant."

Lynn

Do not invite your boyfriend/girlfriend to spend all of his/her time at your place.

"Call it a dirty trick if you want, but I don't care. I couldn't stand Nell's boyfriend hanging around all the time, so I flirted shamelessly with him when she wasn't looking. He got scared and started inviting her over to his place. Works for me!"

Tina

"Tim's girlfriend thought she was making up for coming around every night by cooking and cleaning for us. It drove me nuts. All I wanted was a comfortable bachelor pad and a little privacy. Finally, I blew up at her and asked, *Don't you have a home?* Of course she started bawling, and Tim wanted to pulverize me, so I ended up looking for a place of my own."

Mel

"When Roger and I moved in together, we established the rule that girlfriends can only come over one night a week. I wasn't about to relent to having a non-paying guest around 24 hours a day like the last place I lived. Now I only have to put up with him laying on the couch groping her one night per week."

Paul

Keep your tongue in your own mouth when others are present.

"Watching someone show a little affection is endearing, but Martha and her boyfriend are sickening. They are forever sucking face and it embarrasses me to no end. Keep it in the bedroom!"

Dawna

Don't borrow one another's clothes. One of you will get the elevator; the other is bound to get the shaft.

"My sister Jenny shared an apartment with a girl who had beautiful clothes and plenty of them. She graciously offered her garments to my sister and then in turn would borrow things now and then just to reassure her it was OK to continue imbibing in her closet.

Jenny, under normal circumstances, would have been ecstatic at the opportunity. She and I had borrowed each other's clothes as teenagers, but this situation was different. It seemed that this fashion diva wore outfits several times before laundering or having them dry-cleaned. Thus, she hung my sister's clothes back in her closet soiled, and Jenny couldn't ever find anything clean to borrow from her.

The sad fact remained that my sister didn't have the courage to tell her not to borrow her clothes, so she just ended up with extra laundry."

Wendy

Don't expect to be backed up on anything bigger than a white lie.

No one wants to become entangled in an elaborate web of lies, especially when they aren't your own. And, you don't really want people to think less of you anyway, do you, knowing what manipulative schemes you're capable of? Just keep track of your own little fibs and don't go dragging anyone down the gutter with you.

"Melissa has won the epitome of a perfect man, but she's too immature and wild to handle, or deserve, this relationship. He is a successful professional, climbing his way up a huge salary ladder. She's climbing a ladder too, into the top bunk to sleep with the young guys she parties with at a nearby campus when he's out of town on business. She keeps telling me that this is just a *whim* and she'll outgrow it by the time they get married, but it makes me a nervous wreck.

Just last week, when he was supposed to be working late, he showed up at our door looking for her, with a dozen roses to make up for leaving her alone so much. It is exactly times like these when I get caught having to cover for her. I said I didn't know where she was, but I knew darn well that she was out with one of her hoodlum boyfriends, dressed in an outfit from her secret wardrobe that her fiancée had never seen.

When she showed up, she darted through the door and into the bathroom, leaving her coat on. When she emerged, she was dressed in the same outfit that I had worn to work that day. She had dug my clothes out of the hamper so he wouldn't see the tight pants and midriff top she had had on!

I feel sorry for him, and it makes me furious that she keeps putting me on the spot."

Cherish

Take turns answering the phone and the door.

"Jamie won't answer the phone or the door unless I'm in the shower. I might understand it if she was trying to avoid a stalker or something, but she is just a lazy slug. I bought a new phone will the caller identification feature on it and told her I'd pay the extra charge every month so she couldn't argue about it. Now if I know the call is for *her*, I just ignore it."

Connie

Don't be a know-it-all.

"If I have a great tan, then Gigi knows a hundred people who are dying of skin cancer. If I'm lilly white, then I need to buy the brand of tanning lotion she uses. Please!"

Nicole

"As long as you keep that genius quality under wraps, you'll be appreciated. Thanks to Cheryl, I became the heroine at work when my boss slopped Whiteout down the front of his new shirt. I discreetly called her, and sure enough, she knew he could get it out by soaking it in Alka-Seltzer. Honestly, that girl knows everything, but she doesn't go around blurting it out. She only gives advice when asked."

Connie

Use restraint when overcome by the urge to play the one-upmanship game.

People with a mental edge are usually fun to be around. Whatever you say or do, they seem to be able to add some bit of information to make things more interesting. These people generally make great friends, but when you can't seem to get away from them, especially when you live together, it can be maddening. These clever, Mensa candidates can wreak havoc on your ego.

"This is one of Sami's quirks that makes me crazy. I've stopped telling her anything, because I can't stand it when she immediately tops my story with one of her own. No matter what I've done, she's done it bigger or better, or knows more about it."

Edie

"I searched for what seemed like forever to find the perfect outfit for an engagement party. Terri went out and found the same outfit at an outlet mall for a hundred dollars less. She knew better, of course, than to wear the same thing to the party, but she did exactly as I predicted. She told everyone she heard complimenting me how she had lucked into the same ensemble for much cheaper."

Kathy

Don't expect free counseling.

"What does Brandi think I am, her therapist? She starts in the minute I get up in the morning, griping about everything from her job to a chipped nail. And, if I start to tell her about my problems, she jumps in again as if she hasn't heard a word I've said. Everything is about her. What a narcissist."

Tammy

Don't be a copycat.

A little mimicry can be flattering, but too much can become down right irritating (or unnerving if you've seen *Single White Female*). As with any relationship, you need varied interests and activities or you'll get on one another's nerves.

"I'm the type that has never been bothered by the fear of entering an important social function and finding someone wearing the same dress. Some women are offended by this, and that is exactly why Heather has distanced herself from me. And now, I'm just waiting for her to tell me she's moving out.

She is a clotheshorse, and has excellent taste. She usually empties her shopping bags the minute she arrives home and models everything for me. I couldn't resist one deal she had found, and I went to the same store and bought the same outfit, and subsequently, we arrived separately at a wedding identically dressed."

Beth

"I bought a sports car, so did she. I took a night class; she signed up for it too. I began to collect Barbie dolls, so did she. Even when I'm depressed, she decides she is too. It's like having a little sister that copies everything I do."

Rhonda

Get your own life.

"Does anyone have a life my roommate can borrow? I'm getting so I hate to go home after work because she waits for me like a lonely puppy and then follows me around *everywhere* I go. I can't even run to the corner for a newspaper without her following me."

Nancy

"Regina lives her life vicariously through me now that she's lost her job. She doesn't have a life of her own, so she sits in anticipation of my arrival and wants to know every lousy detail of my day. She says she was fired because she didn't fit the company image. In other words, she was fired because she is a boring pest."

Christine

Don't behave as if you have agoraphobia. Believe it or not, everyone eventually needs a break from you, so go out once in awhile.

"Frank never goes anywhere except to work. He might as well be in prison in solitary confinement. Just once I'd like to have the apartment all to myself instead of coming home to this emotionally needy little pest."

Tim

"It is impossible for me to relate to people who say they hate to come home to an empty house. I'd like to come home and find Joe *not* there. He has friends, but they're always at our place, and if they're not, he's following me around like a puppy, clawing at my heels. I can't even go into my bedroom and close the door without him knocking, wanting to know what I'm doing. Well Joe, if you're reading this, I'm trying to get away from you!"

Doug

When you go out, leave some indication of where you'll be and how long you'll be gone.

You need not explain your whole life away, but if you'll be gone for awhile, it would be courteous to leave a name and number of where you can be reached in case of an emergency. And don't assume others are all that curious about your personal business. Knowing that you're going to be away for a few hours offers the same kind of freedom you had as a kid when your parents went out and finally left you without a babysitter.

"Sally would shoot out the door and not say a word. If I wanted to go somewhere, I wouldn't know whether to lock the door or not. I would anyway and then she'd berate me for locking her out."

Mary

"It would be nice to invite some of my friends over if I knew Marty wouldn't be there. He will disappear for days at a time, and I don't have the foggiest idea where he is. What a creepy feeling."

Adam

"Sammie will get up in the middle of a TV show and just walk out of the apartment. It would be nice to know if he wasn't coming back for awhile so I could watch a movie or something."

Dan

"One day I came home from work and Carly wasn't there, but her curling iron was on, so I figured she must be coming back to get ready to go somewhere. She came back three days later! She'd taken off for the beach and didn't even bother to tell me."

Frannie

Don't feel guilty for not reporting your every move.

Maintaining your independence is one privilege of not living with your parents or not getting married.

"Charlie was a nice guy, but he always had to know where I was and when I would be coming home. I didn't realize the mental hold he had on me until one night when I realized I was driving straight home from work when I really didn't want to. I'd met a girl at work and wanted to ask her to dinner, but I didn't because I had this eerie feeling like I was in high school again and my mom would be waiting for me to come home.

Once I flat out told him how I felt, he butted out of my life."

Darrin

Don't expect everyone to drop all activities at your arrival.

"It was a rare occasion for me to beat Brenda and her boyfriend to the television in the evenings. It was their primary source of entertainment and they weren't very good at sharing.

One evening I was determined to get a well-deserved turn and I parked myself comfortably on the couch and plenty early before they walked in to take the place over.

First, Brenda interrupted me by asking what I was watching. When I told her the name of the movie, she proceeded to summarize the plot in about 30 seconds, said it wasn't any good, and walked over and started flipping channels as she asked, *You don't mind do you?* What a self-absorbed hag."

Lu Lu

No one gets sick on purpose, so show a little compassion by helping out.

"After enduring feverish chills, dry heaves, and a headache for three days, I decided my flu-like symptoms weren't making me a sick as Cheri's attitude towards me. She greeted me the day I dizzily stumbled through the front door after work with, *Oh great, now I'm probably going to get sick.* Well forgive me for being human.

I didn't expect her to come running with a thermometer and a bowl of chicken soup, but she was merciless. The disinfectant she sprayed everywhere was gagging me, and I was forbidden to use the kitchen. I had to wait until she went out just to sneak some broth. How about a little compassion?"

J.C.

Remember: It isn't the magnitude of the favor you ask for, it's the way you ask.

"Why do some people think that living together gives you a license to be impolite? Melanie asked me in an unbelievably snotty tone of voice if I would vacate for the evening. Of course I felt as if I'd done something to make her mad, and I was also curious as to why she wanted me out of the way.

I purposely stalled around, to see what the big deal was. Her parents showed up, and were friendly as always, so I thought she simply wanted a little privacy. Instead of leaving, I stayed in my bedroom and shut the door.

The next morning, she was hysterical. She had wanted to ask them for a loan to get out debt, since she had maxed out her credit cards. She didn't want me to know about it, or to be present for the inevitable ugly scene when she asked — so she didn't. Her parents live three hours away, so she blamed me for screwing up the opportunity to ask for the money.

All she had to do was ask nicely, and I would have been out of the way in a flash."

Angie

Don't pressure anyone into feeling responsible for your social life.

It's no one's fault but your own if your Rolodex is empty. Use your head to develop your own social life. Network through work, clubs, school, church, neighbors, volunteer work, or family members, but not through those you live with unless they initiate something.

"There's no other way to describe Ralph than utterly pathetic. He lives in his recliner pouting because he doesn't have any friends or anything to do, yet we've lived in the same place for two years. The world isn't going to come to him.

I'm not about to invite him along with my friends. I know he'd leech onto us and we'd never get rid of him. He's a nice guy, but he's such a bore."

Jason

"Annie isn't exactly socially progressive, if you know what I mean. She has started hanging around when my new boyfriend comes over and whines about having nothing to do. He is polite to a fault because he has started inviting her along on our dates, and it's becoming maddening because she always accepts. I'm sure that what she really wants is for him to fix her up with a friend, but I'm sure he doesn't know of anyone looking for an emotionally needy girlfriend.

And now, this is just the beginning of the end because she wants to know what we're doing this Saturday and he wants me to lie to her. He wants me to tell her that we're going to his folks, but we're really not. She'll probably find out and there will be a huge blow up. I hate feeling deceitful and I want to tell her the truth, but we don't want to hurt her feelings. Why can't she just buzz off?"

Carrie

Don't be a mother.

"*You're not going to wear that sweater with those pants are you? You ought to get those split ends trimmed. You're not smoking again are you?* Erin drives me stark raving mad with her unsolicited advice. I expect her to start chirping at any moment now, *Don't run with scissors! Your face will freeze like that! You're going to poke somebody's eye out with that!* Geez!"

Renea

"How old do you have to be before you can do whatever you want? I'm forty-five and now I'm living with a woman who sounds like my mother. And she wonders why I'm no longer interested in sex."

Larry

Demonstrate a little sensitivity or stay out of the way during a crisis that doesn't involve you.

"The company I worked for changed hands and within a week, I was out of a job. My unemployment checks wouldn't even touch the bills I had accumulated, so I was frantically searching for another job. I found out just how inconsiderate Judy was during that horrible time in my life. She ignored my request to leave the phone line open, jabbering for hours to her friends. When I finally blew up at her, she stopped. But when I picked up the phone to make sure it was working, I found out she was on the Internet in her bedroom! Eventually I found another job, but thankfully, the commute gave me an excuse to move closer to work."

Terri

"My aunt and uncle lived in an area that was devastated by a freakish flash flood. The phone lines were down and I had no idea if they were OK or not. The only consolation I could find was watching the news for information, but Ben kept complaining that he wanted to watch something else. Well boo hoo."

Travis

Keep your criticism of friends, lovers, or relatives to yourself.

"It's an elementary fact of life that people will defend their relatives, no matter what, even though they may be slugging it out among themselves, and I could have kicked myself for forgetting that. Beth bawls every time she finds her brother's name in the paper for yet another offense, from drunk driving to domestic violence. I made the mistake of announcing that there was another charge listed that she'd missed, and she went completely off on me, calling me a mud-slinging wench."

Kara

"When Julie had a huge fight with her best friend, I thought I'd make her feel better by letting her know my opinion of her. She was nothing but a full-blown control freak who thought she was the only person on the face of the earth who knew how to do anything right. It was such a relief to be rid of her and her unsolicited comments. But about a week later, they made up, and of course, she told her everything I'd said!"

Toni

Never judge the suitability of a romantic interest other than your own.

"In Judy's case, I thought she would *want* to know that Bob had flunked out of college. Now I've alienated both of them and she's moving out."

Misty

"Jenny hates my boyfriend and leaves the apartment when he shows up, or acts like a witch until he leaves. How dare her, trying to control my personal life! I can't wait until the lease runs out so I can get out of here."

Lonnie

If you happen to know some juicy tidbit about your roommate's lover, keep it to yourself.

"Oops. I guess Kevin didn't really want to know that his girlfriend used to be a big rip in high school. They're having a huge wedding and all of our friends are in it except for me, even though I introduced them."

Pete

"When I found out Charlene's boyfriend was married, I was smart about not blabbing it in case she already knew and was keeping it a secret from me. I had someone at work leave an anonymous tip on our answering machine from a pay phone. I was glad she found out and didn't think that I was the one to blow the whistle on him after the confrontation that followed. I certainly didn't want in the middle of that."

Barb

"For weeks, Brenda kept saying, *Wait until you meet the guy I'm dating!* Imagine my surprise when I finally did, and it was someone I'd had a one night stand with months earlier, a mistake I'll never get over. I decided not to tell her, and so far he hasn't either. If he does, I'll deny it to the grave."

Bobbie

"It might sound strange, but I hate Tania for proving that my ex-boyfriend was cheating on me. I think maybe I knew it all along, but I thought I could charm him into dating me exclusively and giving up everyone else. I guess it made me mad because I wasn't ready to let go, yet she kept badgering me and wouldn't let me make up my own mind."

Sandee

"Would someone please tell me why my Jamie felt compelled to tell me she had picked up my boyfriend in a bar before I met him? He was smart enough not to tell me; why wasn't she?

This knowledge changed my entire opinion of her. To me, she is nothing but trash, not because she slept with him, but because she bragged about it. She only wanted to hurt me by intimating that she could have had him first, but didn't want him. Of course that's not the way he tells it, but who knows for sure?"

Kim

Don't interfere with anyone's private agenda.

"Robin was going to a family reunion with her fiancée Brian. He requested that she bake a blackberry pie. She went to the bakery, bought one, and ever so carefully scooped it out of its plain tin pan and into her own fancy pie dish. She passed it off as her own, lattice top and all.

Later that same summer, Brian lost weight. Could she alter his pants to fit again? Why certainly she could. She took them to a seamstress and he never knew the difference.

Even though she is sporting a diamond ring and shopping for a wedding dress, she still maintains an intimate relationship with an old boyfriend. I also know that she may have a physical problem preventing her from having children. She told me, but didn't tell her husband-to-be.

I can't stand knowing that she is such a fraud to the man she is about to marry. Everyone tells me to stay out of it, but it is all starting to work on me."

Lonnie

Expect to meet with some opposition if you have settled into a habitual routine and then suddenly, you break the spell.

"When Karen decided to go on a serious diet, she completely took over the kitchen. Before then, she had eaten out almost every evening and I was able to cook dinner for my boyfriend in peace. What really burns me is that she doesn't even ask if I'm planning on cooking anything. She just waltzes in and crowds me out."

Penny

"Bud is a real socialite and I'm a homebody, so the combination generally works very well, especially since we don't share the same circle of friends. Usually, he just uses the apartment for pit stops, but he recently was charged with DUI, so now he barges in with his rowdy friends and they get drunk at our place. I'm sick of it."

Tom

"When my company cut out my overtime, I didn't miss the money, but I missed the structure of my time. I know I'm driving Morgan crazy because she's used to having the apartment to herself, but I do pay half the rent."

Cindi

Don't whine incessantly.

"You name it, Polly's unhappy about it — her boyfriend, her job, her car, her hair, her flabby thighs, and so on. And what really burns me is that to the rest of the world, she's a fakey little people-pleaser, all sunshine and smiles. Barf!"

Tammy

Don't put others at physical risk.

"Teri is kind of weird in that she lives in some sort of parallel universe. To me, her friends are all faceless. She never goes out, and lives her social life through some Internet chat room. I'm starting to get scared because she's met someone she'd like to date and has talked about inviting him to our apartment. I'd like for her to meet him somewhere else in case he's a creep, but she doesn't seem to be afraid at all."

Mona

Mind your own business.

"How about a little privacy? I'm more embarrassed for Jill than myself when she just comes right out and asks the nosiest questions. *What size cup do you wear? How much do you clear a week? You're not still a virgin are you?* I don't even tell my boyfriend that stuff!"

Julie

"My family is predominantly made up of black sheep, so I don't like talking about them. Laura won't leave me alone, badgering me for the juicy details of their latest escapades.

Recently, my sister was arrested for stalking her husband's lover. Soon after the charge was in the newspaper, she started a demolition derby in the woman's driveway after spotting his car. Do you think I enjoy talking about that kind of thing?"

Jessie

"If I want to call in sick and spend the whole day at the mall, that's my business!"

Terri

Don't be a tattle-tell.

"My mother called one Saturday morning, and Bert informed her I had been out all night and hadn't come home yet. How could anyone be so stupid?"

Ed

"My grandmother came to visit and Betsy kept butting into our conversation to set the record straight. I said my boyfriend and I weren't getting along too well, trying to avoid the worn out premarital sex lecture: *Why would a man buy the cow when he can get the milk free?* Instead of letting it go, she exclaimed, *That's a lie! He's crazy about you!*"

Diane

"Recently, I was hit with a sudden case of explosive diarrhea while pinned between cars waiting in the drive-through line at the bank. I was mortified when I saw my boss strolling across the parking lot, obviously coming right towards me. He tapped on my car window, but I wouldn't roll it down. I said it was broken; he would just have to yell so I could hear him. Then, he opened my car door before I could lock it. It was one of those situations you want to suppress and forget forever. I might as well tell you because Tammy won't shut up about it. She thinks it's hilarious and tells that story over and over."

Bertie

Don't pass judgement unless your roommate's unscrupulous behavior directly effects you.

"Cheri and I are both a perfect size 8, but we never borrow one another's clothes. We're both in our late twenties and the idea seems juvenile to me. My complaint? She buys tons of clothing and wears things only once, then carefully reattaches the tags and returns them.

First of all, in my book, her behavior qualifies as shoplifting. Secondly, knowing that she does this has turned me into a psychotic idiot who sniffs a garment from top to bottom to see if it has been worn before I'll even try something on. I would be furious if I found out I'd purchased something that has already been worn. Her deceitfulness has totally destroyed my trust in her."

Kathleen

"I paid an astronomical price for a summer pass to use the same pool that my roommate hangs out at, and then found out that all the while, she had been sneaking in. She even had the nerve to accept the free drinks served to their patrons and laughed at me saying I was a sucker for paying for a membership. I became a nervous wreck every time we were there together, so I finally called the management and squealed on her on a day when I had to work. They pressed charges, but she is none the wiser, and now I can relax in peace."

Connie

Learn to forgive and forget idiotic mistakes. After all, you will inevitably commit a little faux pas of your own at one time or another.

"I left my car in neutral and it drifted backwards onto our patio and mangled Carol's grill. I thought that once I bought her a new one, she would shut up about it. But no, she has to tell that story everywhere we go to embarrass me.

Finally, I shut her up when I got tipsy at a party and told my own humiliating tale about her. Her five-year-old niece was rummaging through her things and came running out into the living room wearing her bridal veil from her first wedding and innocently asked, *Are you going to wear this one again?* The humorous part was that her new boyfriend was present for the show, and she hadn't told him that she was divorced."

Micki

"Karen kept complaining because her dishes were getting chipped, which I admit I was mostly responsible for, and was willing to replace. Then, I noticed that my grandmother's antique sewing chair was beginning to collapse, and caught her using it as a stepstool. That chair cannot be replaced, so I couldn't care less about her dishes."

Teresa

Express your concerns "before the fact" to head off problems before they occur.

"I laughed so hard, I almost peed my pants when Don came toting his old drum trap set into our apartment. My reaction was enough said. Did he actually think he could play that thing and not stir up the whole building, let alone me?"

Jay

"My biggest fear as a free-lance writer was that June would get on my computer and mess up my files. I didn't want her reading my work anyway, so I just told her I'd rather she didn't touch anything on my desk. Once I said it, I was able to totally relax and stop obsessing."

Chelcie

"When I found a replacement for Denise, I didn't hesitate to tell her everything that previously had driven me nuts. I knew things wouldn't be perfect, but at least it would be something different to deal with."

Dana

Accept that expressing your concerns is not always insurance that you'll get cooperation.

"We agreed to take turns cleaning, but Bob doesn't lift a finger. He thinks sliding the pizza boxes under the couch where no one can see them is cleaning up the living room."

George

"When I divorced and moved in with a friend, I told him how much I hated being married to a hair dresser. She always had hair clinging to her clothes and got it everywhere. It's a wonder I wasn't coughing up hairballs. So I was flabbergasted when his mother stopped by and trimmed his hair right in the middle of the kitchen floor."

Bill

If you're extremely fussy about decorating, you'd better get your own place.

"Annette works at a glass factory and drags home tons of glass figurines and dishes, and sets them everywhere. It reminds me of my grandmother's house, making me feel like a bull in a china shop. I've broken several pieces trying to dust and she won't ever clean. It's probably a matter of *Freudian slips*, if you know what I mean."

Olivia

"What is the point of trying to aesthetically enhance the look of your apartment when your roommate insists on putting an extra roll of toilet paper on the back of the toilet in a crocheted cover topped with pom-poms?"

Lindy

"Our place has the ambiance of a French bordello. Sandee is one of those weird incense burners who loves candles and beaded curtains. At least I'm saving a lot of money now that she has taken over decorating. How can I compete with all this strange stuff?"

Dell

"Without asking if I minded, Cal set up a pyramid of old rusty soda cans by the fireplace that form the outline of Abraham Lincoln's profile."

Jonnie

Forget the old cliché; *Treat others the way you want to be treated.* **It doesn't always apply.**

"You may love the idea of someone cooking a full course meal every night, expressing genuine concern that you eat a balanced diet, all the while not charging you a penny for the groceries consumed. I sure didn't. There were nights that had I not had a steaming side of beef waved under my nose, I would have opted for a lighter, healthier meal, to lessen the damage on my already out-of-control waistline. Nell wouldn't take no for an answer. She thought she was doing me a favor!"

Rebecca

You're too old to have a 4-H project, and human beings aren't on the list anyway. Keep your self-improvement tips to yourself.

"I rarely wear lipstick. It does nothing for the shape of my thin lips and I lick it off or smudge it immediately after application. But Sharon seems to have one goal in life: Making sure I have lipstick on every time I leave the apartment. She claims no woman is completely dressed without it. I have absolutely no backbone, so I've learned to whisk it on, jump in my car, and wipe it off as I drive away. It is easier than listening to her constant nagging.

Now she's starting in on my hairstyle, which she judges as severely out-dated. I believe she sincerely means well, but I know I'll end up hurting her feelings because she just won't give it up and I'm about to blow. She is gorgeous, has a body to kill for, and dresses like a model. I'm older, and tired of obsessively working at my looks. I am comfortable with myself and don't need or want an image consultant."

Trina

"I live with a self-appointed fashion cop, so I feel like I'm sixteen again and trying to sneak out of the house before my mom sees what I have on. I can't take the comments every single day about my hair, clothes, jewelry, and makeup. Give me a break, I work as a secretary in a nursing home!"

Misty

Stop moping around and do something with your life.

"After two years of watching Sally mope around because she got dumped, I finally lost it. People who believe that they only have one perfect soul mate on the face of this earth are crazy. There are probably hundreds of people you'd click with if you'd just get out there and increase your chances of meeting them. No one is going to come banging on your door looking for you.

And why do women think they have to be in love to be happy? You need to fall in love with your life first. No one wants a miserable creature waiting for someone else to be in charge of his or her happiness."

Jenny

If you've got it all, don't flaunt it.

"It has been said that when you hate someone, it is probably because you subconsciously recognize something in that person you dislike about yourself. In my case, it's the reverse. Elina has it all-stunning looks *and* brains, and I have neither. And you know what? I might admire her and even try to emulate some of her success tactics if she were the least bit humble.

I get a complete run down every evening of her day at work. First, we begin by reviewing all the brilliant ideas she introduced to her boss and how he fussed over her afterwards. Then, we see if we can beat the previous day's record for the number of hunks that she had to blow off. What a barf-o-rama."

Veronica

WHEN TENSION BUILDS

(UH-OH. NOW YOU'RE IN TROUBLE.)

No one wants to live in an emotionally charged environment, especially when you seem to be feeling the brunt of someone else's irritability. But before you feign total innocence, take a look at what you're bringing to the party. Most people don't start slamming doors unless there is an obvious problem.

When it's apparent that you're being left to second-guess the cause of a cold war, don't waste time over-analyzing the situation. Everyone paints a different picture, so save yourself some trouble and try to restore harmony by initiating productive dialog. Even if this tactic aggravates him or her into verbally downloading every stinking thing you've ever done wrong, then you've done the job right. Sometimes provoking someone into venting frustrations is enough to put an end to them just by clearing the air.

When this happens, just listen and let it go, because if you attempt to win the fight by making excuses, you won't accomplish anything.

Head emotional turmoil off at the pass by making an attempt to call a truce the minute things get touchy.

"I had such an immature crush on a guy I had just started seeing, I didn't have the nerve to tell him to stop calling me late at night after Susie and I were already asleep. After a couple of weeks of being awakened by the phone ringing, she hit the roof. She didn't speak to me for a week. No matter what I said or did, she just wouldn't melt.

I made a last desperate attempt to make her realize I was truly sorry and to keep her from moving out. I bought a teddy bear and stuck a little white surrender flag under his arm and put it on her bed. Then I told my new beau not to call after eleven.

She took the bait and was finally able to laugh about it."

Wendy

Verbalize why you are angry or get over yourself.

"After weeks of putting up with Andrea's snotty attitude and snide remarks, I made her tell me what was wrong. I had borrowed her dish to take food to a party, and I'd forgotten to bring it home. That was it. That was all she was upset about.

I jumped in the car, drove across town, and got her stupid dish, and that was the end of it. Why didn't she just tell me in the first place?"

Bev

Don't take moodiness personally.

"Lori used to make me feel as if I had done something wrong because she is such a meanie when she is in a bad mood. Now I totally ignore her until she decides she can speak to me in a decent tone of voice. It puts the pressure on her to be nice."

Laura

If you are a moody person, put out the warning before you do any damage.

"When I get up in the morning, I am a total grouch. I don't want to talk to anyone and I don't want anyone talking to me. I told Bethany I've been this way for 25 years, and it's doubtful I'll ever change. The minute she is up, she whistles or sings until she leaves for work. Sometimes I want to reach down her throat and rip her tongue out, but at least she knows better than to try to talk to me now that she knows the drill."

Jerri

"It tickles me that I am not permitted to speak to Jay until after ten o'clock in the morning. He is definitely not a morning person. If I have something to tell him, I write a note and then run away laughing."

Kim

Blame no one but yourself for allowing a bad situation to eat you up emotionally.

There is nothing wrong with justified confrontation; in fact, it can be healthy. Say whatever you need to if it will end your obsessing, but stick to the facts. No need to go on an hour-long tirade. Just say, *You did this or that to me and right now I'm ticked off.*

"I used to pride myself on being a sensitive person, but Shelly made me wish I weren't. She could not allow me one moment of happiness, and I allowed her to make me feel this way. Right before I left on the vacation of a lifetime to Hawaii with my family, she decided to tell me that she wasn't happy about a few things and would have to talk to me about them *later*.

Looking back, I know she was just a green-eyed monster, jealous of my impending trip and wanted to ruin it for me. Well she did, and even though that was five years ago, I could still smack her in the mouth for it. Why didn't I tell her when I had the chance?

When I got back from the trip, she said, *Never mind, I'm over it.*"

Peggy

If you have a complaint, say so before you become so angry you commit an act of retaliation that you will regret.

"Joan held a high ranking position in a bank and participated in any community event that would get her name in the newspaper. Everyone thought she was the most *together* person, except me. Her fast-track life meant that I had to take care of the apartment myself, plus put up with the mismanagement of her personal life. She was so busy, she couldn't take care of even the most meager details.

She had a habit of leaving her car lights on, and then falling into bed too exhausted to hear the neighbors pounding on our door because her lights were shining in their bedroom window. She would spend the night with her boyfriend and leave her alarm clock set for work so it would wake me up on the only day I had to sleep in. I'd find the refrigerator door ajar because she was too busy to take the time to shove something back away from the door.

The last straw was when the hot water faucet in our shower broke and you had to be careful to turn the water all the way off. I got up for work and had about two minutes of luke warm water because she had left the water dripping all night. In a fit of rage, I filled up a trashcan with ice cold water and threw it on her. Of course she whined to everybody about how I scared her out of her wits, so now Miss Perfect is viewed as the victim, not me."

Olive

Don't dig up dead dogs. Do your confronting when you're angry or forget it.

"The entire time Susan and I lived together, she never once uttered a word about anything bothering her. I was flabbergasted, to say the least, when we went our separate ways and she suddenly cut loose with a long list of accusations about how I'd wronged her. Why didn't she say anything while we were living together?"

Polly

"I was sick of Daryl's know-it-all attitude, and it didn't take long for my friends to catch on. If he planned on going out with us, I wouldn't go, and everyone knew why except for him.

One of my best buddies suggested I talk it out with him rather than going to all the trouble of rearranging my life to avoid him. But, we were talking about a personality quirk, not something specific that he had done to me.

Well, you know how guys are. My friends got drunk and told him. He came home, we had a fistfight, and then it was over. He is still a know-it-all, but at least I can call him on it when I feel like it. I should have started speaking up months ago."

John

Be careful about making accusations, especially if you live with only one other person.

When there are just two of you, it is easy to point fingers. Who else could have used the last drop of your shampoo? But sometimes, we shouldn't be so quick on the trigger.

"I thought it was unusually strange how often Amanda's sister stopped by to *pick something up* when I was the only one home. And, I hated the fact that she had a key to our apartment. One time I met her in the parking lot as she was leaving with an armful of clothes. *She'll never miss them*, is exactly what she said.

At the time, it never occurred to me that Amanda might think I was the one ripping her off. After all, how could I steal her clothes and then get away with wearing them?

One night I was at a football game and I saw her storm towards a woman and slap her right in front of the stadium! It was her sister, caught red-handed dressed from head to toe in her clothes.

Later, she related the story to me in an apologetic tone of voice without really saying that she had suspicioned me, but I knew she had. I suddenly remembered her rudely asking several times where I had gotten a gold necklace that looked just like one of her's — the one her sister had stolen."

Alexandria

Don't take totally offensive and narcissistic behavior personally. Chances are, this cretin is driving the rest of the world crazy too.

"Cindi thought so much of herself that she would create parking spaces that didn't exist. It cracked me up when she would drive to the health club, circle the lot, and end up parking on the sidewalk if all the good spots were filled. She did the same thing at our apartment building, parking part way on the lawn with two wheels on the sidewalk, so that everyone had to squeeze around her car to get inside.

One day I just happened to swing open our apartment door in time to catch a glimpse of my neighbor spitting on her windshield. He sheepishly darted into his car and out of the lot. After a little inspection, I observed, yes indeedy, a large hocker and the slimy path it left when it slid down the glass. That ugly scene made me realize I wasn't the only one she irritated."

Liz

"I thought my friends liked Bill, so I always kept my mouth shut when he hung around the apartment, horning in on my social plans. I hated him because he was so cheap and always managed to screw me out of money. One weekend, my buddies and I made reservations to stay in a nice hotel and go to a pro football game. He said he wasn't sure if he could get off work to go, which was a bold-faced lie, so he wouldn't have to commit to paying his part of the deposit.

First of all, he shows up and announces he'll just sleep on the floor of our hotel. Then, we all went to a bar and when it was his turn to buy a round, he decided he was exhausted and went back to the room to crash. When we got back, he was in one of the beds, so I felt obligated to take the floor. After all, he was *my* roommate.

When we were driving home, he crowded into our car because he had hitchhiked to town. But I reached the end of my rope when we drove through a fast food place, and he ordered the most food, and we were five bucks short at the window. Obviously, he had only thrown in a couple of dollars. I called him a social ignoramus and everyone cheered me on as he jumped out of the car. I wish I'd known all along they couldn't stand him either."

Roger

When given the silent treatment instead of an explanation for something you may or may not have done, refuse to feel guilty.

"Nancy would rather run all over the neighborhood telling everyone who will listen what I've done wrong, rather than tell me. How am I supposed to remedy something when I don't know what's wrong? I've made a pact with myself to just ignore her until she pops her cork. Then it's all over in less than an hour. Why doesn't she just tell me to begin with?"

Anne

"The last time I got the silent treatment, it was because the psycho I lived with thought I didn't take a phone message from her sister. After a week of deafening silence, she finally figured out her sister lied about calling to begin with, and admitted it.

I'm sorry, but an apology isn't enough to make up for that kind of treatment."

David

No matter how angry you get, always take the high road.

"Consumed with jealously, I did something so horrific, I had to leave town. I lived in a house with five other girls, and someone moved out, so we needed to find a replacement. Foolishly, I asked a childhood friend I hadn't seen in years to move in. She and I had taken piano lessons from the same teacher growing up, and I never considered the possibility that she would want to play my piano. I became envious when everyone made over how well she played, and it infuriated me because she would bang away while I was trying to watch television or when I wanted to play. I wanted rid of her in the worst way, but everyone else loved her. And, what could I say I didn't like about her anyway, without looking like a jealous idiot?

I started leaving rape threats on her windshield, hoping it would scare her into moving out. That shook her up, but everyone ran to her emotional rescue. Then, I flattened one of her tires, but a neighbor saw me do it and called the police. I've never been so humiliated in my entire life. Everyone knew instantly I'd written the notes too."

Beth

Don't waste your time fighting with a control freak about trivial issues.

"I read everything I could get my hands on to find out what makes a control freak tick, and then I learned how to deal with Celia. It seems that she wasn't trying to be mean to me, she was just desperate to reduce her own anxieties by trying to make her little universe perfect. Armed with this knowledge, it made it easier to let her have her way about things that didn't really matter. I knew she was probably mad about something bigger that she couldn't control.

She got angry when I didn't fold up a newspaper perfectly and put it in the hundred-dollar basket she bought for the fireplace, but it didn't take much probing to find out what was really going on. She exploded with the information that she was embarrassed when her snooty friends were over because our furniture is so old. She can never enjoy anything she buys because she concentrates on what she *doesn't* have."

Laura

No matter how bad things get, resist the opportunity to get revenge by bringing up embarrassing subjects in front of company.

"I don't know what Tammy hopes to gain from this, but she blatantly reveals things to my boyfriend and friends that are clearly none of her business, and are just plain unnecessary barbs.

Did you know Lisa's old boyfriend called? Can you believe she ate an entire gallon of ice cream in two days? Did you know she quit her aerobics class?

And who knows what she's really mad about."

Lisa

"It is no secret that Julie can't stand me after living together for a year, but she had no business introducing me to her new beau as a *puzzle enthusiast*, and in a condescending tone of voice to boot. I have only put together one puzzle the entire time I've lived with her, and it was to entertain my seven-year-old niece. That snot-face just wants to make sure he won't introduce me to any of his friends and risk having to socialize with me."

Jo Ann

"I had just finished my first day of work at a real job, as an engineer, when my new boss called to see how I felt about my new position. My twerpy, immature roommate picked up the other line to ask if I could hurry up and get off the phone, making me look like a little kid."

Gary

Don't put up with cruel behavior. Take positive, yet fair action.

"Once Barb became engaged, I thought I could ride out the time before the wedding even though she and her fiancée had pretty much taken over the apartment. I had to spend my evenings elsewhere, stay in my room, or feel awkward sitting on the floor to watch TV because they were either hogging the furniture, or had things piled up so you couldn't sit down.

I usually came home at night just in time to go to bed and check my phone messages. The closer to the wedding date, the fewer messages I would find. Then, a casual acquaintance sheepishly asked why I hadn't returned his calls, and I became suspicious.

Soon after, I noticed a piece of paper in the trash with my name on it. I pulled it out and it was a phone message. She had been innocently taking messages while her fiancée was present, trying to look like the nice little bride-to-be, and then she was throwing them away! Apparently she had grown to hate me, for reasons unknown to me, and who knows what other tricks she'd been pulling.

The phone was in my name, so I had it disconnected immediately and bought a cell phone. It was the best thing I ever did. She practically disappeared because she had to be somewhere else where she could use a phone to firm up her wedding plans."

Toni

Forget about trying to even the score. You'll surely end up the loser.

"My heart was pounding when I found Laurel and my boyfriend waiting for me to get home from work. I was scared to death someone had died or been in a terrible accident, but my heart was racing for the wrong reason. They were waiting to tell me that they had been suffering for months because of their undeniable attraction for one another, and decided to finally break the news to me.

I thought I'd get revenge by telling her parents, face-to-face, what she'd done to me. They already knew and were happy about it! Boy, did I look like a raging lunatic."

Peggy

"My bother's best friend was a police officer. When he found out Joyce had poured rubbing alcohol in my contact case before I moved out, he wanted me to file a report. Luckily, I had smelled her little transgression before applying my lenses, and they were disposable anyway, so no real harm had been done. But, *she* didn't know that, so he paid her a little visit in uniform. Who needs the bogeyman when you know a good cop?"

Amanda

"My boyfriend, Pete, and I were postponing announcing our engagement so we wouldn't detract from the attention Heather was enjoying during her upcoming marriage. So much for being nice. She made me miserable our last few weeks together. Evidently, she thought some of my property was fair game as an extra send-off gift. I also had to repaint her bedroom to get back our security deposit.

In spite of being angry with her, I still played the part of an attentive bridesmaid truly wishing her well. But then she made the mistake of telling someone during the wedding reception that Pete would never marry me, that he was just using me for sex. When he saw that I was ready to cry and found out why, he grabbed a microphone and proposed right in front of everyone.

Of course that went over like a turd in the punch bowl, so I told her our original plan and that I was glad Pete didn't follow through with it."

Laurie

Vow to channel the energy from your anger into doing something positive for yourself.

"One of the rewards of being a high school teacher is knowing you have made a difference in a child's life, especially when it goes beyond academics. One of my ex-students, who will be a sophomore in college, bragged to me that she is getting better grades than she earned in high school and is banking most of the spending money her parents and grandparents send her. A former spoiled brat, Kari says she owes her success and new-found modest living style to the roommate she had her freshman year and to me for preaching about making productive, not destructive, choices in life.

Apparently, Kari had met her match with this self-absorbed minx. She wore her clothes without asking, used up all of her necessities, loaned out CD's that didn't even belong to her, and snitched her cash. The obvious answer would have been to move, but she hated to leave the terrific new friends she'd made on her floor, and there weren't any openings anywhere nearby. So, she devised another plan to deal with this heretic's insufferable behavior.

During Christmas break, Kari took her stereo, good clothing, and everything she didn't need to survive home. She brought back a heavy metal box with a lock on it for her money and necessities, and wore the key on a chain around her neck. She wore jeans and comfortable T-shirts under flannel shirts she borrowed from her dad. With her simplistic new life-style, she became introspective and truly interested in her education.

In addition to her growing bank account and improved grades, she was rewarded this year by being chosen as a resident assistant in her dorm. Besides getting free room and board, she will also have a huge room and private bath, all to herself.

She admitted that before leaving for the summer, she swiped one of the old witche's shirts and intends to wear it around campus next year just to get back at her. But the bright side is that she has decided to continue on this austerity program until she graduates, and then use the money to tour Europe before she starts working."

Ben

When the going gets tough, try *killing your roommate with kindness.*

"I offered to do everything I possibly could to make Karen happy. I never said anything that wasn't in a genuinely nice tone of voice, and I never looked at her without smiling. Eventually she cracked. She couldn't resist my new attitude and I benefited by starting to feel the way I was act-ing. We became closer and are still together after five years."

Peggy

"My wise Jewish grandmother said something to me that made me real-ize I was the one causing the tension. She asked, *How could anyone not like you?* I realized I did not speak or behave around Suzette the same way I did around my sweet grandmother."

Amber

Don't think you have to move out every time something goes wrong.

When a problem arises, your best bet is to get it out in the open and try to work it out. If you jump the gun and start packing every time things don't go your way, you're only going to exchange one set of problems for another.

"What a relief it was to move away from home. My mother took care of all the cleaning and laundry, but she controlled my life. After I moved in with my friends, I had all the freedom I wanted, but I was the only domesticated animal in the apartment. Then I got married so I could turn the Molly-Maid stuff back over to a woman, but she tied me to the bedpost.

That lasted about three years, and then I moved in with another guy tainted by a bad marriage. His kids wrecked the place, and he thought *Comet* was only something in orbit, so I was stuck again holding the toilet bowl brush — but by golly I could have a beer whenever I wanted to.

After I got rid of "Oscar Madison" and his brats, I decided to get my own place. Now I'm lonely. Is anybody out there looking for a place to live? I've got an extra bedroom."

Fred

Preparing For the Aftermath

(Put away that arsenic and read on.)

So you've discovered you've made a poor choice in a roommate. You are no longer able to make concessions, unintentionally causing your already wilting relationship to go completely awry. You want out, and you want out now. But keep your head, so that when it's finally over, you don't go down in flames.

Even if you are certain you are about to part ways, aim to remain cordial in case you'll still be in contact. At the very least, you will need to settle up final bills. But more importantly, treating one another with mutual respect is the decent and grown up thing to do.

When you are in a predicament that seems void of solutions, make sure the escape route you choose doesn't cause repercussions you can't live with.

"Moving out in the middle of a lease caused more problems than it solved. Instead of trying to find a replacement like she said she would, Sally stabbed me in the back by whining to the landlord that I'd bailed. He filed on me in small claims court so I had to keep paying rent while she enjoyed a spacious apartment."

Cammie

"Peggy was mad I'd *inconvenienced* her by moving, so she wrote my parents a letter, asking for my share of the final bills, saying I wouldn't pay up even though she'd never even asked me. She also told them every dirty detail of my private life. They know I'm not perfect, but the way she embellished everything nearly destroyed me in their eyes."

Terri

"I volunteered for mission work in Zimbabwe to get out of a bad situation. Who do you think was punished for that choice? At least I didn't have to worry about getting my turn in the bathroom — there wasn't one!"

Brenda

Maintain your integrity in your final days together. Acts of revenge are likely to give you only temporary relief.

"Toni and I were data entry clerks at the same bank, and that, coupled with living together, just didn't work out. We had little spats for over a year, and when she accused me of letting her cat out on purpose, I knew it was time to part company. That stupid animal tried to escape every time the front door opened, and she knew it wasn't my fault.

Soon after that, our supervisor called me into her office because that gasbag was blabbing all kinds of tales about me to other employees. She asked me if there was some kind of problem, but I kept my cool and said I would prefer to keep my private life at home. In reality, I would have liked nothing better than to have unloaded right then and there, but I didn't. The next thing I knew, I was moved out of the maze of cubicles and into an office with a window. The hefty raise I received with this move certainly softened the blow."

Diana

If you allow yourself to avenge shabby treatment, make it something harmless that gives you smug satisfaction, rather than risk doing malicious, irreparable damage.

"Meredith was viciously jealous of my popularity, so when she got married, she asked some of my girlfriends, whom I had introduced her to, and not me, to be in her wedding. Then, she twisted the knife by taking them shopping for the wedding, having little luncheons, seating them at the family table at her bridal shower, and whatever else she could do to make me feel excluded from the celebration.

At the reception, an older woman who lived next door to us followed me into the bathroom to tell me how flabbergasted she was when she saw that I was not in the wedding. I burst into tears, prompting her to suggest I get a little innocent revenge. She said, *You're not going to let 'em see you cry honey.* Dinner hadn't even been served yet, but she and I slipped out to go to a bar and get plastered.

My friends told me later that it drove Meredith crazy looking for me. The most loyal of the bunch told her that if she was so intent on me being present for the whole affair, she should have asked me to be in the wedding."

Tracey

When anticipating a potentially ugly departure, maintain your composure to avoid a scene. Nothing lasts forever.

"Thank God Anna was getting married because our relationship had deteriorated beyond repair. I sincerely didn't care when she constantly paraded her bridesmaids and wedding paraphernalia around the apartment, even though she was doing it to rub my nose in the fact that I wasn't a part of the wedding.

When that didn't seem to ruffle my feathers, she took desperate measures. She had her fiancée recruit my boyfriend as an usher and callously reminded me that I wouldn't be sitting at the head table for dinner, nor would I be invited to the rehearsal dinner. Then, she decided to cut back the guest list *for economic reasons*, and didn't invite any of our mutual friends to insure I'd feel the sting of being completely left out.

Of course she left the apartment a wreck when she moved out, but I continued to hold my head high and kept my mouth shut. I attended the wedding as if nothing were out of the ordinary and mingled with complete strangers.

I'm proud of myself for being able to rise above her behavior, and exit gracefully from our relationship. In fact, I've heard through the grapevine that even her own sister questioned her cruelty towards me."

Renea

Keep track of what you accumulate so there won't be any question of what belongs to whom on moving day.

"A divorce would have been easier because you expect to negotiate over who gets what and you have the legal system to support you. Tammy just boxed up what she wanted and split. She robbed me blind. To this day, I'll start looking for something and realize that she swiped it."

Robin

Let go of your anger, or let go of the relationship.

"Even though the words were never spoken, Bobbi and I despised each other by the time she finally got married and moved out. I made one last attempt at being civil by attending the ceremony, but I still couldn't keep my emotions under total control. The gift I bought was an intentional insult. I spent five dollars on an ugly glass figurine at a flea market.

A few weeks later, she came back at me by insinuating my cheapness by claiming that she hadn't written me a thank-you note yet because someone must have switched the cards on some gifts. She said my card was stuck on the most idiotic thing you ever saw that some old lady friend from her church must have purchased. Why doesn't she just leave me alone?"

Pricilla

You're living in a free country, so exercise your right to absolve a living arrangement with a nut.

"I could overlook Nancy's obsession with allowing a psychic to dictate her every decision, as long as it didn't interfere with my life. It was when she started talking about having had cyber sex on my computer that I hit the floor running to find another place to live."

Karyn

"Jodi fasted for 13 days to lose weight for her high school class reunion. On the eve of the big event, she discovered she'd lost so much weight her shoes were too big. She begged me to run to the mall to find an identical pair of shoes in a smaller size so she wouldn't have to shuffle around all evening. Then, she called from the reunion, and wanted me to have her paged so everyone would think she was important. And at two o'clock in the morning, I had to go fetch her from the emergency room because she'd passed out from drinking on top of starving herself for two weeks.

This was just a typical day with her, and it was wearing me out. I'm afraid if I move she won't be able to take care of herself."

Bonnie

Even if you part amicably, be prepared for negative repercussions if you shared the same circle of friends.

"Not long after I moved, I made the decision to make a clean break from my circle of friends. I didn't want to, but one of us had to go, and asking a clique to choose between you is so *junior high school*. In the three years we lived together, Shelly and I never fought, but you could cut the tension with a knife. Envious of my success at work and the money I made, she had started disclosing intimate details about me, just to humiliate me.

Specifically, she kept alluding to the fact that I had a mechanical sex toy, which she knew darn well was a back massager I'd gotten after getting rear ended in traffic. *What were you running in there at night? Sounded like a jackhammer. Ha, ha, ha.* Then I ended up looking like the junkyard watchdog when I took offense to her comments because *she was just kidding me.*"

Karen

When you move out, don't leave anything behind.

Don't think you're being generous by leaving a trail of unwanted items. If you don't want something, then you can bet nobody else wants it either. It is a deceitful trick to pack up and split without cleaning up after yourself.

"I filled three garbage bags with the trash Missy left behind. I threw them in my car, drove over to her new apartment, and emptied the contents in a huge pile in front of her door."

Janna

"A month after I was settled in a new apartment, my old landlord called telling me to empty the storage bin or I wouldn't be getting my deposit back. I didn't *have* anything in the storage bin. When I checked it out, there were boxes and boxes of cheesy baseball souvenirs from the factory where my ex-roommate worked. Apparently, he had stolen them thinking he'd resell them, but then changed his mind and was too lazy to do anything with them. I returned them to the factory, told them where they came from, and I could care less what happened to him."

Beau

Demand what's yours, but let the small stuff go.

"The minute we started talking about going our separate ways, Val began laying claim that *this was her's and that was her's*. I got scared that she would take something precious of mine, so I cleaned out a couple of filing cabinet drawers at work and hid things there. There was no way she was taking off with anything my grandmother had left me, especially her silverware. The rest of the junk, she could have."

Barbie

Don't disgrace yourself by not paying your share of the final bills.

Even if the lease and utilities weren't in your name, why damage your reputation by duping your ex-roommate by not paying up?

"When Sally got married, I never dreamt she wouldn't pay me for her share of the final month's rent and utilities. I was so angry I ended up calling her husband to see if perhaps he would feel the responsibility to cough up the money. This only made a bad situation worse.

Out of no where, she came up with this story that she had indeed paid me. She said she had been foolish to give me cash because she knew I would try and pull this dirty little trick, and I was just jealous of her. All of this came after I'd shelled out mega bucks for shower and wedding gifts, and a lecherous bridesmaid outfit."

Melanie

"I'm nobody's patsy. I reminded Fred in front of his mom that he still owed me five hundred bucks. He knew he'd have to pay me for fear I'd bring it up again."

Herb

"My old roommate skipped town when I was away for the weekend. I went to the post office and filled out a Freedom of Information form, giving our old address. They gave me his forwarding address and I tracked him down and made him pay up."

Kyle

Make sure you have a plan before you bail out.

If the arrangement isn't working and you know it never will, start making plans. The less time you have together once the cat's out of the bag, the less time you'll have feeling miserable.

"Unbeknownst to me, Robin unplugged the phone to take a nap and forgot to hook it back up, or so she says. For two days, I sat by the phone waiting to be called for a second interview for a job I was so confident I'd get, I'd already quit my old job. Needless to say, the job went to someone else, and I was furious. I'd already announced I was moving and now I couldn't because I couldn't afford my new apartment without that job.

It was four long months before I could find something else and afford to move. During that time, I was living off of my savings and didn't feel like I could even go out for a cup of coffee because I didn't know how long it would take me to find employment and get back on my feet. I might have been able to get past her wretched behavior, but she acted as if she had been the one wounded!"

Shara

Don't plan on throwing anyone out on the street. Allow ample time for arrangements to be made.

"On May 28th, Jon told me his girlfriend was moving in on June 1st. Most of the furniture was mine, but she had her own stuff, so he wanted me out in three days. What a three-ring circus. I couldn't find an apartment I could afford and I didn't have access to a truck anyway.

They moved all of her things in anyway, and we lived in what felt like a storage bin for two months. If he would have let me know earlier, I would have been searching for a place immediately."

Ben

Use firmness and finality when announcing it's over.

If the arrangement isn't working and you know it never will, then don't Mickey-mouse around. Announce your plan and get on with it.

"I took a wrong turn when I said I was *thinking* about moving out. Betsy started a campaign to try to fix whatever was wrong. *Is it because my sister hangs around too much? Am I hogging the bathroom? Am I too sloppy?*

If I started listing every inconsiderate thing she had ever done, she would probably get mad. And if I didn't, she would be living in a state of constant paranoia. I was just ready for a little privacy."

Danielle

If you are stuck in a rotten arrangement for awhile, try to salvage something good out of the time you have left.

Nothing lasts forever, but it may feel like it when you're waiting for the lease to run out, or some other milestone to free you, like graduation or a wedding. Make the waiting go faster by deviating your routine or cramming your schedule in a way that will turn the negative into a positive for you.

"To pass the time and get out of the apartment in the evenings, I joined a gym. I'm in the best shape I've ever been in."

Darren

"Do what I did. I took a part-time job at a mall working evenings and weekends. With the employee discount and the extra money I made, I built up a wardrobe to die for."

Beth

"Having a horrible roommate was the best thing that ever happened to me. I started working on my master's degree at night just to get out of the apartment, and was able to finish in a year and a half. If she had been nice to me, I never would have accomplished this."

Diana

"The only way I could find to deal with it was to stay in my bedroom and escape into a fantasy world by reading novel after novel. Then, I discovered this fantastic book club and met a ton of new friends, and found someone compatible to move in with."

Miranda

"Because I started volunteering for as much overtime as I could possibly get, I was able to pay off my car, save a pile of cash, and stay out of the house while doing it."

Paul

"The situation ended up enabling me to advance my career. My boss began viewing me as an overachiever because I was working over every night to avoid going home. I got a huge promotion out of it and was able to afford my own place."

Randy

"I made friends with an elderly woman in our building who needed errands run and help around her apartment. I figured since I was miserable,

I'd try to make someone else happy. And, when things were tense, I could run to her place and get away for awhile."

Tommie

"She ate my food, wore my clothes, and ruined what little furniture I had. I began spending as little as possible, buying only the bare essentials. If I did splurge on something like a new outfit, I would hide it in the trunk of my car with everything else I didn't want her pawing through. By the time I moved out, I had quite a nest egg in the bank."

Michelle

Don't blame your "ex" for wanting to be happy.

"Haley was not only my maid of honor at my wedding; she was also the best roommate I ever had. Leaving her to get married was more traumatic than having Opie, my first dog, put to sleep. We started out sharing a dorm room the size of one of my current clothes closets, and then graduated from apartment to apartment as our incomes steadily increased. By the end of our twelve-year relationship, we had perfected the rules of cohabitation, or so I thought.

Soon after returning from my honeymoon, I called to see how my replacement was working out. Haley's only concern seemed to be surviving the 132 days left on the lease so that she'd be free of the extra-terrestrial currently occupying my old bed. I reminded her that we were not always perfect for each other. We had to work at it from time to time. Then she hung up on me!

Had she forgotten how long it had taken to train me not to shove every dish we owned under my bed, the dog I offered to sit that nearly got us thrown out, and the countless phone messages I failed to write down and then forgot about? And just when our relationship was finally as close to perfect as you can get, I accidentally fell in love. So, I opted for marriage, which meant negotiating all over again with someone new, only this time it would be permanent. So Haley wasn't the only one scared."

Penny

Don't get too torn up about parting ways. Maybe you didn't get along as well as you thought.

"Becky and I remained friends for awhile after she got married, but I had to end our relationship because of the emotional pain she began to inflict upon me. Why didn't she tell me when we were living together all the things she hated about me? Her tally of everything I had done to her was endless and extremely petty. I felt as if I hadn't known her at all, but roomed all that time with a total stranger."

Cindy

"My ex-roommate spilled her guts the day she moved out. Apparently, she didn't want anything to do with me ever again. Life's too short, so I say, *Bygones*."

Tammi

0-595-12983-8

Printed in the United States
19487LVS00008B/18